نقاء السلافة في أحكام البيعة والخلافة

THE SACRED LINK.

The Sacred Link.

شيخ الإسلام الإمام أحمد رضا خان القادري

ALA HADRAT IMAM AHMAD RIDA KHAN

Translated by Mufti Sayyid Abdul Samad al-Qadiri

TheSunniWay

THE SACRED LINK.

contact@thesunniway.com

ISBN: 978-1-957773-19-3

إِنَّ الَّذِينَ يُبَايِعُونَكَ إِنَّمَا يُبَايِعُونَ اللَّهَ يَدُ اللَّهِ فَوْقَ أَيْدِيهِمْ

Verily, those who pledged allegiance to you have pledged allegiance to Allāh Himself – the hand belonging to Allāh is over their hands.

SŪRAH AL-FATḤ [10]

لَقَدْ رَضِيَ اللَّهُ عَنِ الْمُؤْمِنِينَ إِذْ يُبَايِعُونَكَ تَحْتَ الشَّجَرَةِ

Certainly, Allāh was pleased by the believers when they would pledge allegiance to you beneath the tree.

SŪRAH AL-FATḤ [18]

DEDICATED TO

My shaykh

Tāj al-Sharīʿah

Badr al-Ṭarīqah

The Chief Qāḍī of Hind

The Successor of al-Muftī al-‘A`ẓam

The Lamp of Guidance in our Dark Era

The Jurist • The Author • The Mufassir • The Muḥaddith

The Muḥaqqiq • The Mudabbir

MUFTĪ SHĀH ‘AKHTAR RIḌĀ’ KHĀN AL-‘AZHARĪ

al-Qādirī • al-Barakātī • al-Riḍawī • al-Nūrī

رضي الله عنه

INTRODUCTORY COMMENDATION

By Qa'id al-Millah Mufti Asjad Rida Khan

بسم الله الرحمن الرحيم

Allāh's name to commence, the Most Compassionate, the Ever-Merciful.

All praise is due to Allah Almighty, and blessings and peace be upon His Beloved Prophet *(ṣalla Allāh 'alayhi wa sallam)*.

The blessed pen of my great ancestor, the Reviver of the Fourteenth Century, Ala Hazrat Imam Ahmad Raza Khan Alayhir Rahmah, produced works of immense value and timeless relevance. His treatise نقاء السلافة في أحكام البيعة والخلافة is among those treasures that clarify crucial matters of allegiance and leadership in Islam.

I have been informed that Mufti Sayyid Abdul Samad Sahib of Maryland has undertaken the translation of this work into English. I wholeheartedly commend this noble effort, which renders the original text accessible to a wider audience, enabling more seekers of knowledge to benefit from its wisdom. May Allah grant this endeavour acceptance, make it a means of guidance, and bestow abundant reward upon all who contributed to its publication.

والله ولي التوفيق

Faqeer Muhammad Asjad Raza Khan Qadiri

(Markaz-e Ahle Sunnat Bareilly Shareef)

19th Safar Al-Muzaffar 1447H | 14th August 2025

FOREWORD

By Mufti Faizan ul-Mustafa Qadiri

بسم الله الرحمن الرحيم

Allāh's name to commence, the Most Compassionate, the Ever-Merciful.

The writings of Sayyidī 'A`lā Ḥaḍrat, may his secret be sanctified, are no less than food for the soul for those passionate of knowledge. Upon reading just a few pages, the eyes find light, and the hearts find contentment – the soul becomes rejuvenated.

Before me is a vital treatise concerning *bay'ah* and *'irshād* (spiritual allegiance and guidance), and it is incumbent upon the people of *bay'ah* and *'irshād* to study this. This treatise is a compilation of several edicts *(fatwas)* of 'A`lā Ḥaḍrat, may his secret be sanctified. The important issues related to general *khilāfah*, exclusive *khilāfah*, spiritual successorship, spiritual allegiance, and spiritual guidance have been gathered in this. In this, the derivation of 'A`lā Ḥaḍrat, may his secret be sanctified, from the texts of the *fuqahā'* (jurists) and the scholars of *Ḥadīth* for the chain of reliability of spiritual successorship is brilliant. Moreover, the derivation 'A`lā Ḥaḍrat, may his secret be sanctified, has exercised in the matter of renewing the allegiance to the original guide on the hands of the exclusive representative from the report of Sayyidunā Ṭalḥah, may Allāh be pleased with him, is deeply moving. Those interested should read this time and time again.

The question is oft-asked concerning the statement of the Noble *Ṣūfīs* that, "The *shaykh* of the one without a *shaykh* is *Shayṭān*," and 'Alā Ḥaḍrat has clarified this exceptionally well.

My dearest and most upright, 'Allāmah Muftī Sayyid 'Abdul Ṣamad, may Allāh Almighty preserve him, has translated this treatise into English diligently and left no deficiency in its organizational and developmental fronts. Upon this beautiful presentation, I congratulate him sincerely, and I ask Allāh Almighty to accept his efforts and to make his role in conveying and publishing the teachings of Riḍā' a model for generations to come, *'Āmīn*.

Faqīr Faizān ul-Muṣṭafā Qādirī
University of Imām 'Abū Ḥanīfah and Tāj al-Sharī'ah Islamic Institute (Lucknow)

Muḥarram al-Ḥarām 21, 1447 H.
July 17,2025

ENDORSEMENT

By Mufti Afthab Cassim al-Qadiri

بسم الله الرحمن الرحيم

Allāh's name to commence, the Most Compassionate, the Ever-Merciful.

نحمده و نصلى و نسلم على رسوله الكريم و آله وصحبه
الكرام أجمعين و من تبعهم بإحسان إلى يوم الدين

All Praise is for Allah Almighty, Who created Man in the Best of Moulds, thereby granting him Dignity, And Spiritual Capacity.

Durood and Salaams upon the Greatest in the Creation, the Soul of Humanity, and the Greatest Ocean of Spirituality; Sayyiduna Muhammad Mustafa *(ṣalla Allāh 'alayhi wa sallam)*, the Nabi of every Nabi, and upon the Ahle Bayt and every Sahabi, Whose Blessed Hands are in the Sacred Hands of Allah's Beloved Nabi *(ṣalla Allāh 'alayhi wa sallam)*, Especially upon Abu Bakr, Umar, Uthman, and Ali, Whose sincere Allegiance to Him *(ṣalla Allāh 'alayhi wa sallam)* opened the doors for the Allegiance of Loyalty, thereby granting them all the Pleasure of Allah Almighty.

You have before you the English translation of *Naqā' al-Salāfah fī 'Aḥkām al-Bay'ah wa al-Khilāfah*, the masterpiece of Sayyidi Aala Hazrat Imam e Ahle Sunnat Ash Shah Imam Ahmed Raza Khan Qaadiri Barakaati Radi Allahu Anhu, which discusses the Laws of Spirituality related to the Grand Spiritual Allegiance of Loyalty.

This meticulous work of the great Imam has been translated beautifully into English by Mufti Sayyid ʿAbdus Samad Al Qaadiri Razvi Noori of Maryland (USA), who has been doing exceptional service for the Deen and the Maslak, alongside his enthusiastic team of Mufti Sayyid Asad Al Qaadiri Razvi Noori and Mufti Salman Noori at Muslim Dreamers and Aminah Islamic Center.

I have only managed to browse through the book briefly, as I have been travelling and am currently in Madina Shareef, the City of Radiance and Spirituality. I was very pleased with what I read, and I am confident that this book will be of great benefit to the seekers on the path of Spirituality. It will also serve to protect the Sunni masses from charlatans who approach unwary seekers in the guise of being spiritual masters, whereas such individuals do not qualify for this esteemed position due to their contravention of the Shari'ah and the Sacred Laws of Spirituality.

It is my humble Dua, through the Wasila of Nabi Kareem *(ṣalla Allāh ʿalayhi wa sallam)*, that Almighty Allah grants acceptance to this translation, and showers Mufti ʿAbdus Samad and his team of Ulama and supporters with even greater acceptance and prosperity in both Deen and Duniya. May He keep them, and us all, firm with steadfastness upon Maslak e Aala Hazrat. *Aameen.*

MASLAK E AALA HAZRAT - ZINDA BAAD!
TAAJUSH SHARIAH FOREVER

SAG E MUFTI E AZAM
Muhammad Afthab Cassim Qaadiri Razvi Noori
Imam Mustafa Raza Research Centre (Durban, South Africa)

15 Muharram 1447 Hijri
Currently in Madina Shareef

PUBLISHER'S NOTE

By Mufti Zahid Hussain al-Qadiri

بسم الله الرحمن الرحيم

والصلاة والسلام على رسوله الكريم صلى الله عليه و على آله وصحبه أجمعين

I am certainly pleased that Sayyid Mufti Abd al-Samad Sahib has provided the English speaking world with the book, 'The Sacred Link' which is a translation of Naqā' al-Salāfah fī 'Aḥkām al-Bay'ah wa al-Khilāfah by the great Mujaddid Imam Ahmed Raza.

Sayyid Mufti Abd al-Samad Sahib is the head of TheSunniWay, Maryland, USA. He is a sincere and authentic scholar and propogator of the Maslak of Imam Ahmed Raza which is the true Ahl al-Sunnah Wa al-Jamaa'ah. He is a Khalifah of Qaid al-Millah Sheikh Mufti Asjad Raza Khan who is currently the head of the Markaz in Bareily Shareef. He is a loyal student of Mufti Faizan al-Mustafa Qadiri who is a grandson of Sadr al-Shariah Allamah Amjad Ali Aazmi.

Sayyid Mufti Sahib has provided many beneficial books to the English readers, I am certain he will add to this list in the future. I pray that people benefit from his hard work and that Allah rewards him immensely for his service. May he continue to excel in his services for the Deen.

Faqeer Zahid Hussain Qadiri

PREFACE

By The Translator

بسم الله الرحمن الرحيم

Allāh's name to commence, the Most Compassionate, the Ever-Merciful.

الحمد لله رب العالمين مطلوب الطالبين ۞ الذي نور طريق الاهتداء بالمرشدين ۞
والصلوة والسلام على إمام الأنبياء والمرسلين ۞ رحمة للعالمين مراد المشتاقين ۞
وعلى خلفائه الراشدين ۞ من آله الطيبين الطاهرين ۞ وأصحابه الهادين المهتدين ۞
والآخذين طريقهم إلى يوم الدين ۞ وعلى الشيوخ الصالحين ۞ من الطريقة العلية
العالية القادرية البركاتية الرضوية النورية أجمعين ۞ خصوصا الغوث الأعظم عبد القادر
سيد السالكين ۞ وإمام المسترشدين ۞ أحمد رضا مجدد الملة والدين ۞ أما بعد

The work before you is a translation of a treatise regarding a number of rules and laws of Ṣūfism, or spirituality in the religion of 'Islām, by the name of *Naqā' al-Salāfah fī 'Aḥkām al-Bay'ah wa al-Khilāfah* penned by the *'Imām* of the *'Ahl al-Sunnah*, *'Imām* 'Aḥmad Riḍā' Khān al-Qādirī, may Allāh sanctify his secret. This treatise is a collection of eight separate queries sent to the noble *'imām* which the *'imām*, as per his habit, answered with utmost diligence while demonstrating his unparalleled mastery in yet another science.

Unarguably, the impact of 'A`lā Ḥaḍrat's, may Allāh sanctify his secret, pen in any field is that it delivers satisfaction to the reader. This is the reason that no matter how well studied a scholar may be in any particular field, upon conclusion of their research, they study the works of the noble *'imām*, and if their research coincides with the conclusive research of the *'imām*, they find solace in publishing their work. If they find their own research to be in disagreement with the *'imām*, a sincere scholar's eyes are opened to the flaws of his own research and efforts, and he seeks to understand the subject at hand from the works of the *'imām* in order to rectify himself. Keeping this in mind, one can truly see the significance and vital importance of a text penned by the *'imām* concerning the spiritual and inward path of *'Islām*.

'A`lā Ḥaḍrat, may Allāh sanctify his secret, though recognized by most for his expertise and unparalleled mastery as a jurist, is also a celebrated *ṣūfī*, one who represents the path of spirituality as was represented by the pious men of the previous eras. This is truly evident in his influence as a *shaykh* and guide to his disciples. The seekers who received attention from the court of the noble *'imām* are highly renowned for becoming perfect guides themselves, and the perfection instilled into the disciples by a guide is the mark of the *shaykh's* own perfection. After their *shaykh*, his students and disciples displayed exemplary competence and conveyed his mission and message without flaw.

May Allāh Almighty be pleased with each one of them and may He reward them on our behalf for delivering the message of the *'imām* to us without any alteration.

In the current era of widespread misinformation, the pure path of the noble *ṣūfīs* has been a target of unjust representation. Some can be seen propagating a disfigured version of *ṭarīqah* which caters only to the *nafs* and ego – one that frees man from the boundaries and limitations of the laws given by Allāh Almighty – while others reject the totality of Ṣūfism, depriving themselves and others from the fruits this blessed path brings.

Moreover, of those claiming to be the representatives of Ṣūfism, many are found to be opposing the sacred laws of the *sharī'ah* while merely wearing the guise of *ṭarīqah* – painting an image that the *sharī'ah* is but a road to spirituality, and that the road there is not of any need once the destination has been reached.

On the other hand, a true representative and wayfarer of this sacred path, the beloved *khalīfah* of 'A`lā Ḥaḍrat, Sayyidunā Ṣadr al-Sharī'ah Muftī 'Amjad 'Alī al-'A`ẓamī, may Allāh sanctify his secret, writes, "*Ṭarīqah* is not a contradiction of the *sharī'ah*. It is the spiritual (bāṭinī, inward) portion of *sharī'ah* itself. What the few ignorant pseudo-*ṣūfīs* often say, that '*Ṭarīqah* is one thing and *sharī'ah* is another,' is utter misguidance, and to consider oneself unbound by [the constraints of] the *sharī'ah* based on this erroneous assumption is explicit kufr and heresy."[1]

The laws of the blessed *sharī'ah* are to be followed by every mature and sane believer. To say that one who attains the prize of *wilāyah* is no longer obliged to follow these rulings is sheer ignorance. *Wilāyah* is a position granted to those closest to Allāh Almighty, and to counter the *sharī'ah* is the behavior of those disobedient to Allāh Almighty. He who disobeys the Creator Almighty cannot be the one beloved to Him.

Sayyidunā Ṣadr al-Sharī'ah, may Allāh sanctify his secret, further writes, "No *walī*, no matter how great he may be, can be excused from exercising the laws of the *sharī'ah*. Some imbeciles who rave that, 'Sharī'ah is the route. The route is needed by those who are yet to reach the destination. We have arrived!' Sayyid al-Ṭā'ifah, the Honorable Junayd Baghdādī, may Allāh be pleased with him, says to them:

---

[1] *Bahār e Sharī'at, Vol. 1, Chapter of Wilāyah, Belief 2*

صدقوا لقد وصلوا ولكن إلى أين إلى النار

They speak the truth, they have reached.
However, to where? To the hellfire!" [2]

The renowned jurist, Muftī 'Amjad 'Alī, may Allāh sanctify his secret, then goes on to describe a certain group of people who, due to their state which apparently displays a loss of touch with reality, are excused from acting upon the *sharī'ah*, "However, if the sanity which bears the burden of *sharī'ah* (*'aql taklīfī*) has gone away due to *majdhūbīyah* (the state of being a *majdhūb*, a *walī* who seems to have lost his sanity but is deeply immersed in the remembrance of Allāh Almighty), similar to the one who has fainted, then the pen of the *sharī'ah* will be lifted from him. However, this too shall be understood: the one who is of this category, he will never speak in this manner. He will never challenge the *sharī'ah*!"[3]

Many a pseudo-*ṣūfī* today contradicts the *sharī'ah* by his word and action, yet when reprimanded for his antics, he pays no regard to that which the *sharī'ah* has ordained. Due to such corruption in the name of Ṣūfism, the first introduction many receive of it is of some alien religion which promotes music, dancing, free mixing of the genders, and at times the usage of drugs and alcohol, Allāh Almighty forbid. Thereupon, it is this first impression that pushes the sensible away from such a concept, but to the point that they, being unaware of the origins of Ṣūfism, reject the idea completely. Instead of learning that Ṣūfism or *Taṣawwuf* is in fact the idea of perfecting one's practice of the blessed and pure *sharī'ah*, they fall victim to the deceitful notion that this is a concept contradictory to the mighty law of Allāh Almighty.

---

[2] *Bahār e Sharī'at, Vol. 1, Chapter of Wilāyah, Mas'alah 3*

[3] *ibid*

Furthermore, the first challenge that man faces upon learning of and embarking upon the path of *ṭarīqah* is the search for a *shaykh*. This too is no easy feat. Man will encounter many who claim to have reached great heights of this mountain, yet, at the end of his search, he will find that those who abstain from such haughty claims are the ones truly worthy of *bay'ah*.

The treatise at hand addresses several questions that someone new to the realm of *Taṣawwuf* (Ṣūfism) may face, but the detailed explanations given in the responses by the noble *'imām* make the work a great resource for scholars as well. This treatise is a compilation of eight separate queries presented in the court of the noble *'Imām* 'Aḥmad Riḍā', may Allāh sanctify his secret. The various topics in the eight responses include:

1. The significance and importance of attaching oneself to a chain which connects him to the Messenger of Allāh, may blessings and salutations be upon him

2. The various categories of the *khilāfah* (successorship)

3. The importance of adhering to only one *shaykh* alone

4. The ruling on the individual who does not subscribe to any particular *ṭarīqah* or chain of allegiance

5. The proof of establishing successorship, or *khilāfah*, for any disciple of a *shaykh*

6. The qualities necessary for a *shaykh* to possess to be deemed worthy of allegiance

7. The process of renewing the allegiance after the passing of one's *shaykh*

8. The role of a *shaykh* being exclusive to the male gender

I pray that Allāh Almighty makes this work as beneficial as the original writings of the noble *'imām*, may Allāh sanctify his secret, and that Allāh Almighty makes it a means of strengthening my own connection and link with my *shuyūkh*. Furthermore, I ask Allāh Almighty that He make this work of the noble 'A`lā Ḥaḍrat a means of reform amongst those who are mere claimants of treading this blessed path of spirituality.

This work would not be possible except with the love and support of my teachers, my seniors, my brothers, my spouse, and the sincere supporters that Allāh has bestowed unto me in the form of students. May Allāh Almighty reward them all in abundance.

***Faqīr* `Abdul Ṣamad al-Qādirī,**
may he be pardoned

October 31, 2023
Rabī` al-Thānī 15, 1445 H.

Table of Contents

TABLE OF CONTENTS

The First Question

THE FIRST QUESTION

Blessings of the Muhammadan Chain

QUERY SEVENTY-NINE *Jumādā al-'Ūlā 25, 1318 H.*

Zayd says, "I am a Muslim born to Muslims – since birth, an adherent to the *'Ahl al-Sunnah wa al-Jamā'ah* upon the way of *'Islām*. I am equipped to debate against any baseless claim of another path that contradicts the *Sunnah*. That which a *Shaykh* informs of – he informs of it from the *Qur'ān* and *Ḥadīth*. I already know these things and I already enact them. However, even if I do not – we will rise amongst the followers of His Sanctified Eminence, may Allāh Almighty send blessings and salutations upon him, on the Day of Resurrection, so what need is there for pledging allegiance or committing to a spiritual chain?"

Give a concise response to this ignorant notion so that this satanic whisper becomes distant from the heart, and so we may repent and perform *'istighfār* in the future.

Explain and be rewarded!

THE ANSWER

Sharī'ah, Ṭarīqah, and Ḥaqīqah are all in the Qur'ān

The *sharī'ah*[4], *ṭarīqah*[5] and the *ḥaqīqah*[6], are all found in the *Qur'ān* and *Ḥadīth*. The most prominent of them and the easiest are the matters of the *sharī'ah*. Their state is such that if the *mujtahid 'imāms* had not explained them, the *'ulamā'* would have failed to understand, and had the noble *'ulamā'* not explained and clarified the statements of the *mujtahid 'imāms*, then us people would fall short of even comprehending the statements of the *'imāms*. Furthermore, if today, the people of knowledge do not detail the meanings of the books before the laymen and do not coordinate the [accurate] ruling with a specific case, then the laymen would surely and certainly prove to be incapable of extracting the rulings from the books; they will commit mistakes in a thousand places and understand one thing to be another. Thence, this system exists – that the laymen hold fast onto today's people of religious knowledge, they, in turn, to the texts of the expert scholars, they onto the scholars of *fatwā*, they onto the *'imāms* of guidance, and they onto the *Qur'ān* and *Ḥadīth*.

Blind is he who breaks this chain. Whoever leaves the grasp of the guide from his hand will soon fall into a deep well.

The Sublime *'Imām*, the Gnostic of Allāh, Sayyidī 'Abd al-Wahhāb Sha'rānī, may his holy secret be sanctified, states in *Mīzān al-Sharī'ah al-Kubrā*:

---

[4] *Sharī'ah: the divine law which governs all aspects of life (translator)*

[5] *Ṭarīqah: the path of inner purification and spiritual discipline which aims to perfect the application of the laws of the sharī'ah (translator)*

[6] *Ḥaqīqah: literally means "reality" – it is a spiritual state in which one comes to unveil the deeper realities of existence and recognize Allāh (translator)*

لو قد أن أهل الدور تعدوا من فوقهم إلى الدور الذي قبله لانقطعت وصلتهم بالشارع ولم يهتدوا لإيضاح مشكل ولا تفصيل مجمل وتأمل يا أخي لولا أن رسول الله صلى الله تعالى عليه وسلم فصل بشريعته ما أجمل في القرآن لبقى على إجماله كما أن الأئمة المجتهدين لو لم يفصلوا ما أجمل في السنة أبقيت السنة على إجمالها وهكذا إلى عصرنا هذا إلخ

If the people of an era bypass those [directly] above them to the era which is before them, their reach to the Legislator [upon him be blessings and salutations] will certainly be broken and they shall neither find guidance to the clarification of the ambiguous nor to the detailing of the vague. And contemplate, my brother! Had the Messenger of Allāh, may Allāh send blessings and salutations upon him, not detailed with his sharī'ah what is concise in the Qur'ān, it would surely have remained upon its ambiguity – just as if the mujtahid 'imāms did not detail what is concise in the Sunnah, the Sunnah would have remained on its ambiguity, and so forth to this era of ours...[7]

Also, in this [text] is:

كما أن الشارع بين لنا بسنته ما أجمل في القرآن وكذلك الأئمة المجتهدين بينوا لنا ما أجمل في أحاديث الشريعة ولولا بيانهم لنا ذلك لبقيت الشريعة على إجمالها وهكذا القول في أهل كل دور بالنسبة للدور الذين قبلهم إلى يوم القيامة فإن الإجمال لم يزل ساريا في كلام علماء الأمة إلى يوم القيامة ولولا ذلك ما شرحت الكتب ولا عمل على الشروح حواش كما مر

Just as the Legislator [may blessings and salutations be upon him] clarified for us through his Sunnah what is ambiguous in the Qur'ān, the mujtahid 'imāms clarified for us what is vague in the prophetic narrations of the sharī'ah. Was it not for their clarification of that for our sake, the sharī'ah would have remained upon its ambiguity. The same is to be said concerning the people of every era in relation to the era which precedes them up until the Day of Resurrection. For indeed, the ambiguity continuously travels throughout the words of the scholars of the nation until the Day of Resurrection. Had that not been so, the books would not be given commentaries, nor would those commentaries be provided marginalia as has been mentioned [previously].[8]

---

[7] *al-Mīzān al-Kubrā, Faṣl wa mimmā yudilluka 'alā Ṣiḥah 'Irtibāṭ Jamī' 'Aqwāl 'Ulamā' al-Sharīfah*

[8] *al-Mīzān al-Kubrā, Faṣl fī Bayān 'Istiḥālah Khurūj Shay'*

The Non-*Muqallids* went astray upon breaking this chain and failed to recognize that:

ہمہ شیران جہاں بستۂ ایں سلسلہ اند
روبہ از حیلہ چساں بگسلد ایں سلسلہ را

Every lion of the world is bound by this chain,
How can the fox weaken this chain with its trickery?

The Need of a Shaykh

When this is the state of the rulings of the *sharīʿah*, then it is clearly manifest just how impossible it is to derive the subtleties of *sulūk*[9] (spiritual wayfaring) and the realities of Islamic Gnosis (*maʿrifah*) from the *Qur'ān* and *Ḥadīth* on one's own without the means of a perfect guide (*murshid kāmil*). This path is extremely narrow and without the lantern of a *murshid* (spiritual guide) – how many a great man the accursed *Shayṭān* has beat on this path to the point that he delivered them to the netherworld.

Who are you to walk in it without a perfect guide and claim to pass through it unharmed?

The noble ʿ*imāms* say, "No matter how great of a scholar or ascetic man may be, it is incumbent (*wājib*) upon him to take a gnostic *walī* as his guide. Without this, there remains no way. It is stated in *Mīzān al-Sharīʿah*:

فعلم من جميع ما قررناه وجوب اتخاذ الشيخ لكل عالم طلب الوصول إلى شهود عين الشريعة الكبرى ولو أجمع جميع أقرانه على علمه وعمله وزهده وورعه ولقبوه بالقطبية الكبرى فإن لطريق القوم شروطا لا يعرفها إلا المحققون منهم دون الدخيل فيهم بالدعاوى والأوهام وربما كان من لقبوه بالقطبية لا يصلح أن يكون مريد القطب إلخ

---

[9] *Sulūk: the way or path of a spiritual seeker (translator)*

Thus, learned from all of what we stated is the necessity of taking a shaykh for every scholar who desires the access to the witnessing of the reality of the grand sharī'ah, even if all of his contemporaries agree upon his knowledge, his practice, his asceticism, and his piety, and they confer unto him the title of Grand Quṭbīyah[10]. For indeed, there are conditions for the path of the [ṣūfī] people that none but the researchers amongst them recognize, and not those included amongst them by [mere] claims and assumptions. Moreover, the one conferred the title of Quṭbīyah is often not even worthy of being the disciple of a [true] quṭb..."[11]

This is for the one who wishes to tread this path. Even if the undetermined and lazy are undesirous of *sulūk* (spiritual wayfaring), they still require a *shaykh* to act as an intermediary to Allāh.

Despite Allāh being sufficient for His slaves, Allāh Almighty says:

أَلَيْسَ اللَّهُ بِكَافٍ عَبْدَهُ

Is Allāh not sufficient for His slave?[12]

The Glorious *Qur'ān* commands:

وَابْتَغُوا إِلَيْهِ الْوَسِيلَةَ

Seek a medium towards Him (Allāh).[13]

[10] *Quṭbīyah: A station in wilāyah which literally translates to "axis-hood" – it is the station of the quṭb, around whom the 'awliyā' revolve (translator)*

[11] *al-Mīzān al-Kubrā, Faṣl 'Anna al-Qā'il Kayf al-Wuṣūl*

[12] *Sūrah al-Zumar: 36*

[13] *Sūrah al-Mā'idah: 35*

Reaching the Prophet Without a Medium

The medium to Allāh is the Messenger of Allāh, may Allāh send blessings and salutations upon him, and the medium to the Messenger of Allāh, may Allāh send blessings and salutations upon him, are the noble *mashā'ikh* – link after link. Just as the reach to Allāh, Mighty and Sublime is He, without a medium is *muḥāl qaṭʿī* (definitively impossible), reaching the Messenger of Allāh, may Allāh send blessings and salutations upon him, without a medium is practically difficult.

It is proven through prophetic narrations that the Messenger of Allāh, may Allāh send blessings and salutations upon him, is the intercessor and will be an intercessor in the court of Allāh, Mighty and Majestic is He. In his court, the *'ulamā'* and *'awliyā'* will intercede for their adherents.

The noble *mashā'ikh* aid their disciples in the world, the hereafter, the struggle of death, the grave, the grand assembly (*ḥashr*), and in every situation. It is stated in *Mīzān al-Sharī'ah*:

قد ذكرنا في كتاب الأجوبة عن أئمة الفقهاء والصوفية أن أئمة الفقهاء والصوفية كلهم يشفعون في مقلديهم ويلاحظون أحدهم عند طلوع روحه وعند سؤال منكر ونكير له وعند النشر والحشر والحساب والميزان والصراط ولا يغفلون عنهم في موقف من المواقف إلخ

We have mentioned in Kitāb al-'Ajwibah 'an 'A'immah al-Fuqahā' wa al-Ṣūfīyah that the 'imāms of the fuqahā' and the ṣūfīs, all of them, intercede for their adherents. They observe each of them at the time of their soul being lifted, his questioning from Munkar and Nakīr, resurrection (nashr), the grand assembly (ḥashr), the account, the scale [of deeds], and the bridge (ṣirāṭ). They are not negligent of them in any situation...[14]

[14] *al-Mīzān al-Kubrā, Faṣl fī Bayān Jumlah min al-'Amthilah al-Maḥsūsah*

Who is more of a fool and an enemy to their own well-being than the dependent without hands or feet who does not take a helper even at the time of their calamities?

It is in a *ḥadīth* that the Messenger of Allāh, may Allāh send blessings and salutations upon him, says:

استكثروا من الإخوان فإن لكل مؤمن شفاعة يوم القيامة

Seek a great number of brothers, for indeed, to every [perfect] believer belongs [the right of] intercession on the Day of Resurrection.

'Ibn al-Najjār narrated it in his *Ta'rīkh* from 'Anas bin Mālik, may Allāh be pleased with him.[15]

The Blessings of His Link

Moreover, in the case that nothing else was to happen, Allāh forbid, is the blessing of a continuous chain to the Prophet, may Allāh send blessings and salutations upon him, so insignificant for which even to this day, the noble *'ulamā'* attain the chains of transmission for *ḥadīth* – such that they even seek blessings from the chains of Ratan Hindī, etc.?

'Imām 'Ibn Ḥajar 'Asqalānī says in *'Iṣābah fī Tamyīz al-Ṣaḥābah*:

أنبئت عن المحدث الرحال جمال الدين محمد بن أحمد بن أمين القشهري نزيل المدينة النبوية في فوائد رحلته أخبرنا أبو الفضل وأبو القاسم بن أبي عبد الله بن علي بن إبراهيم بن عتيق اللواتي المعروف بابن الخباز المهدوي فذكر بسنده حديثا عن خواجه رتن قال وذكر خواجه رتن بن عبد الله أنه شهد مع رسول الله صلى الله تعالى عليه وسلم الخندق وسمع منه هذا الحديث ورجع إلى بلاد الهند ومات بها وعاش سبع مائة سنة ومات لسنة ست وتسعين وخسمائة وقال الأقشهري وهذا السند يتبرك به وإن لم يوثق بصحته

[15] *Kanz al-'Ummāl: 24642*

I was informed by the migrating muḥaddith, Jamāl al-Dīn Muḥammad bin 'Aḥmad bin 'Amīn al-'Aqshahrī, the resident of the Prophetic City, in his travelogue, "'Abū al-Faḍl and 'Abū al-Qāsim bin 'Abū 'Abd Allāh bin 'Alī bin 'Ibrāhīm bin 'Atīq al-Lawātī, alias 'Ibn Khabbāz al-Mahdawī, informed us..." He then mentioned his chain of narration from Khwājah Ratan and said, "Khwājah Ratan bin 'Abd Allāh mentioned that he indeed witnessed [the battle of] Khandaq with the Messenger of Allāh , may Allāh send blessings and salutations upon him, and heard this ḥadīth from him. He returned to the lands of Hind and passed away in them. He lived for seven hundred years. He passed away in the year 596 (H.). 'Aqshaharī says that blessings are sought from this chain of transmission despite its authenticity being uncertain." [16]

Virtues of the Ghawth

Thereupon, what can be said about the chains and mediations of the noble *'awliyā'* – particularly the soaring and lofty chain of His Luminous Eminence, Sayyidunā Ghawth 'A`ẓam, the universal *quṭb*? May Allāh send blessings upon his noble grandfather, his noble forefathers, and upon him. He who has stated, "My hand is over my disciple as the sky is above the Earth." [17]

He also says, "If my disciple's foot slips, I will grab their hand."[18]

This is the reason as to why His Eminence is referred to as *Pīr Dastagīr* (the *shaykh* who grabs the hand).

[16] *al-'Iṣābah fī Tamyīz al-Ṣaḥābah, Ḥarf al-Rā', al-Ra' ba'dahā al-Tā', 7866: Ratan bin 'Abdullāh*

[17] *Bahjah al-'Asrār, Dhikr Faḍl 'Aṣḥābihī wa Bushrāhum*

[18] *ibid*

He also says, “If my disciple is in the east while I am in the west and his veil is opened, I will close it.”[19]

He also states, “I have been granted a register wherein as far as the eye can see are the names of my disciples until *Qiyāmah,* and it was said to me:

وهبتهم لك

I have granted all of them to you.” [20]

رواها عنه الأئمة الثقات رضي الله تعالى عنهم وعنا بهم آمين والله تعالى أعلم

The reliable *'imāms,* may Allāh Almighty be pleased with them and with us for their sake, have narrated these [reports] from him. *'Āmīn.* ***Allāh Almighty knows best.***

---

[19] *ibid*

[20] *ibid*

The Second Question

THE SECOND QUESTION

Categories of the Khilāfah

QUERY EIGHTY *1297 H.*

Sent by His Luminous Eminence Mawlānā Ḥaḍrat Sayyidunā Shah 'Abū al-Ḥusayn 'Aḥmad Nūrī Miyāñ Ṣāḥib Māhrehrawī, may his blessings be prolonged.

This query was for some clarification regarding the *khilāfah* (authority of representation) and the *sajjādah-nashīnī* (successorship) of the noble *'awliyā'*. Its objectives are evident in the contents of the response.

THE ANSWER

الحمد لله والصلوة والسلام على حبيبه المصطفى وآله الكرام السادات
الشرفا وصحابته العظام والأولياء العرفاء وعلينا معهم دائما أبدا

All praise is for Allāh. Blessings and salutations be upon His beloved, the Chosen One, and upon his noble progeny, the eminent masters, and upon his sublime companions, and the gnostic 'awliyā', and upon us alongside them, forever and always.

Thereafter, the *khilāfah* of the noble *'awliyā'*, may Allāh deliver to us the benefit of their blessings in this world and the hereafter, is of two types: *'āmmah* (general) and *khāṣṣah* (exclusive).

Khilāfah 'Āmmah (General Khilāfah)

'Āmmah: is that whoever the *murshid murabbī* (the spiritual guide who also gives spiritual training) sees to be honest and capable of facilitating training amongst his closest and distant *murīds* (disciples), he makes them a *khalīfah* and representative. He also grants a similitude of *khilāfah* to authorize him to accept allegiance *(bay'ah)*, to prescribe to him the *'adhkār* (recitations), *'ashghāl* (traditions), *'awrād* (litanies), and *'a'māl* (practices), and also for him to train those who desire it and guide those who seek guidance.

This meaning [of *khilāfah*] is strictly a religious position, and in this, to have more than one *khalīfah*, without any limit or extent, is permissible and effective. All of the noble companions of His Eminence, the Master of all Creations, the Guide of all, Muḥammad al-Muṣṭafā, may Allāh send blessings and salutations upon him, in this meaning, were *khulafā'* (pl. of *khalīfah*) of His Eminence, and it is this very *khilāfah* that has been regarded the inheritance of the Prophets. Moreover, in this meaning, the scholars of the religion, the perfect *shuyūkh* (pl. of *shaykh*), and the people of the *sharī'ah* and *ṭarīqah* up until the establishment of *Qiyāmah*, are all the *khulafā'* and representatives of the Honorable Messenger, upon him be the most superior blessing and commendation. Furthermore, this *khilāfah* can coexist alongside the lifetime of the bestower of the *khilāfah* – as is apparent.

Khilāfah Khāṣṣah (Exclusive Khilāfah)

Khāṣṣah: is that following the passing of the *murshid murabbī*, this individual ascends their exclusive seat upon which none other than him were permitted to sit on in his lifetime. A position will be established for him in all affairs of organization, order, control, management, dismissal and appointment of staff, the expediting and delaying of affairs, authority over the endowments of the *khānqāh*, and the establishment of the *khānqāh's* expenses.

This meaning, although in reality is related to religion, on the surface, it is related to the temporary world (*dunyā*).

Just as Sayyidunā 'Alī, may Allāh Almighty ennoble his countenance, said regarding the *khilāfah* of Sayyidunā ['Abū Bakr] al-Ṣiddīq, may Allāh be pleased with him:

رضيه رسول الله صلى الله تعالى عليه وسلم لديننا أ فلا نرضاه لدنيانا

The Messenger of Allāh, may Allāh Almighty send blessings and salutations upon him, was pleased with him for our religion. Shall we not be pleased with him for our dunyā (worldly life)? [21]

[21] *al-Ṭabqāt al-Kubrā li 'Ibn Sa'd, Dhikr Bay'ah 'Abū Bakr*

This *khilāfah* is very similar to the grand *khilāfah* and *'imāmah* and thus, cannot coexist with the lifetime of the bestower of the *khilāfah*. This is exactly what a spiritual successor is.

In this regard, foremost consideration will be given to the explicit mention of the bestower of *khilāfah*. Whoever he has appointed as the heir apparent or for whomever he has issued a bequest near the time of passing will be appointed on the condition that the bequest is considerable in the *sharī'ah*, that the heir who has been mentioned is worthy and deserving, and that if any endowments are attached to the *khānqāh*, he possesses competence of authority over them. In the presence of this, the case is not to be referred to the advisory council and the authorities (*'ahl al-ḥall wa al-'aqd*) under the assumption that the explicit dictum – which is accepted and considerable in the *sharī'ah* – is insufficient, similar to how it is in the case of the grand *'imāmah* and grand *khilāfah*.

Moreover, mere tacit agreement and lack of negation will surely not be considerable against the explicit dictum, and more so when the dictum is more recent. For example, if someone in the presence of the *murshid murabbī* says, "After his eminence, Zayd will be the successor," or if the writing of any individual contains such content and is recited in the presence of the *murshid murabbī*, and he remains silent upon hearing such a statement or writing. Then, following this, he issues the bequest of successorship in the name of 'Amr, or in the partnership of Zayd and 'Amr, then only this bequest will be admissible, and that [previous] silence will continue to fall short of the threshold of consideration.

والدليل على ذلك قاعدتان من الفقه الأولى لا ينسب إلى

ساكت قول والأخرى أن الصريح يفوق الدلالة

The evidence for that is two principles of fiqh: the first is that a statement shall not be attributed to the silent[22]*, and the other is that the explicit [statement] outweighs implication.*[23]

In the case that two explicit dictums are discovered and in one, the explicit mention is a bequest in the name of Zayd, and the second in the name of ʿAmr, or for both, and the date of one of them is later than the other, then even then, both dictums will remain valid, and Zayd and ʿAmr both will be deemed heirs. However, if the latter dictum is a withdrawal of the prior dictum, and the prior heir has been dismissed, then undoubtedly, the latter will abrogate the prior.

This is as it is in Radd al-Muḥtār regarding the etiquette of heirs, [related] from *Tātārkhānīyah:*

أوصى إلى رجل ومكث زمانا فأوصى إلى آخر فهما وصيان في كل وصاياه سواء
تذكر إيصاه إلى الأول أو نسي لأن الوصي عندنا لا ينعزل ما لم يعزل الموصي
حتى لو كان بين وصيتيه مدة سنة أو أكثر لا ينعزل الأول عن الوصاية

[If] someone makes any man an heir and stayed for some time, then made another an heir, then both are heirs in it all (all of his affairs) whether he remembers his bequest in the name of the first or has forgotten, because according to us, the heir is not dismissed except if dismissed by the one appointing the heir, such that if there is a gap of one year, or more, between both of his bequests, the first will not be dismissed from being the heir.[24]

In the case that there is no dictum, then the historical tradition of the *dargāh* and *khānqāh* will be adhered to, or whoever the authorities come to a consensus upon.

---

[22] *al-ʿAshbāh wa al-Naẓāʾir, al-Fann al-ʿAwwal, al-Qāʿidah al-Thāniyah ʿAshar*

[23] *Radd al-Muḥtār, Kitāb al-Nikāḥ, Bāb al-Mahr*

[24] *Radd al-Muḥtār, Kitāb al-Waqf, Faṣl Yurāʿī Sharṭ al-Wāqif fī ʿIjāzatihī*

However, in these two scenarios, it is imperative that the aforementioned individual possesses *khilāfah ʿāmmah* from the *murshid murabbī* by acceptable means. Otherwise, even if by means of assuming responsibilities or, due to the absence of a *qāḍī* in our lands, by the consensus of the people, the authority of the endowments is validated – the successorship will surely not be valid as that is *khilāfah khāṣṣah* (exclusive khilāfah), and no *khāṣṣ* (exclusivity) can be established in absence of *ʿāmm* (generality). Moreover, *khilāfah ʿāmmāh*, by any means, cannot be attained without valid authorization (*ʻijāzah ṣaḥīḥah*).

Seven Types of Khilāfah[25]

The honorable ʻAsad al-ʿĀrifīn Sayyidunā wa Mawlānā Ḥadrat Sayyid Shāh Ḥamzah ʿAynī Mārehrawī, may Allāh Almighty sanctify his pure secret, states in his Bayāḍ Sharīf:

معلوم باد کہ خلافتِ مشائخ کہ دریں ولایت مروج ست بر ہفت نوع ست بعضے ازاں مقبول
بعضے ازاں مجہول اول اصالۃ دوم اجازۃ سوم اجماعا چہارم وراثۃ پنجم حکما ششم تکلیفا ہمفتم اویسیا

It should be known that the khilāfah of the mashāʾikh (pl. of shaykh) which is prevalent in this region is of seven types: the first is ʻiṣālah, the second is ʻijāzah, the third is ʻijmāʿ, the fourth is wirāthah, the fifth is ḥukm, the sixth is taklīf, the seventh is ʻūwaysī.

I. ʻIṣālah (Direct Spiritual Appointment)

اما اصالۃ آنکہ بزرگے بامر الٰہی شخصے را خلیفہ خودگیر وجانشین خودگر داند

As for ʻiṣālah, it is that any shaykh appoints his khalīfah and successor based on the command of Allāh.

[25] *Note: Sayyidunā ʿAʿlā Ḥaḍrat, upon him be mercy, lists all seven types of khilāfah, but details only five of them. (translator)*

أقول وذلك كما في الحديث عنه صلى الله تعالى عليه وسلم ما قدمت ابا بكر وعمر ولكن الله قدمهما وعنه صلى الله تعالى عليه وسلم سألت الله ثلاثا أن يقدمك يا علي فأبى علي إلا تقديم أبي بكر وقال صلى الله تعالى عليه وسلم يأبى الله والمؤمنون إلا أبي بكر إلى غير ذلك من الأحاديث

I say: That is as it is in the *ḥadīth* from him, may Allāh Almighty send blessings and salutations upon him, "I did not give precedence to 'Abū Bakr and 'Umar, but Allāh granted them both precedence."[26] Also from him, may Allāh Almighty send blessings and salutations upon him, is, "I beseeched Allāh three times that He grants you precedence O 'Alī. He refused to me except the precedence of 'Abū Bakr."[27] He, may Allāh Almighty send blessings and salutations upon him, said, "Allāh and the believers refused any but 'Abū Bakr,"[28] and up to others from the *'aḥādīth*.

II. 'Ijāzah (Authorization)

رجعنا إلى كلام سيدنا حمزة قدس سره العزيز واجازة آنكه شيخ مريدے را خواه وارث خواه بيگانه قابل كار ديده برضا ورغبت خود خليفه كرد

We resume the word of Sayyidunā Ḥamzah, may the Dominant sanctify his secret: And 'ijāzah is that a shaykh deems any disciple fit for the task, whether he be an heir or not, and authorizes him as his khalīfah by his own pleasure and interest.

أقول كاستخلاف أمير المؤمنين حسن بن علي رضي الله تعالى عنهما

I say: Like 'Amīr al-Mu'minīn's (Sayyidunā 'Alī) appointment of Ḥasan bin 'Alī, may Allāh Almighty be pleased with them both, as the *khalīfah*.

---

[26] *Kanz al-'Ummāl: 32666*

[27] *Kanz al-'Ummāl: 32637*

[28] *Kanz al-'Ummāl: 32583*

III. 'Ijmā' (Communal Designation)

[Continuing the word of Sayyidunā Ḥamzah 'Aynī, may Allāh be pleased with him:]

واجماعا آنکہ شیخ ازیں عالم نقل کرد کسے را خلیفہ نگرفت
قوم و قبیلہ وارثے یا مریدے را بخلافت دے تجویز نمایند

And 'ijmā' is that the shaykh passes away from this realm without having appointed a khalīfah, and so the people of the nation and tribe appoint the heir or a disciple as the successor of the shaykh.

أقول كاستخلاف أهل الحل والعقد أمير المؤمنين علي كرم الله
تعالى وجهه بعد شهادة أمير المؤمنين عثمان رضي الله تعالى عنه

I say: Like the authorities' appointment of 'Amīr al-Mu'minīn 'Alī, may Allāh Almighty ennoble his countenance, as the khalīfah after the martyrdom of 'Amīr al-Mu'minīn 'Uthmān, may Allāh Almighty be pleased with him.

[Continuing the word of Sayyidunā Ḥamzah 'Aynī, may Allāh be pleased with him:]

اما ایں خلافت نزدیک مشائخ را نیست وایں نوع خلافت را خلافت اختراعی گوید

This khilāfah, according to the mashā'ikh, is not prevalent, and this type of khilāfah is called khilāfah 'ikhtirā'īyah (fabricated khilāfah).

أقول لانعدام الخلافة العامة المشروطة لصحة الخلافة الخاصة في باب الطريقة أما علي
كرم الله تعالى وجهه فقد كان من أجل خلفاء رسول الله صلى الله تعالى عليه وسلم

I say: Due to the absence of *khilāfah 'āmmah* which is a condition for the validity of *khilāfah khāṣṣah* in the field of *ṭarīqah*. As for 'Alī, may Allāh Almighty ennoble his countenance, he is amongst the most sublime *khulafā'* (pl. of *khalīfah*) of Allāh's Messenger, may Allāh Almighty send blessings and salutations upon him."

IV. 'Wirāthah (Hereditary Succession)

[Continuing the word of Sayyidunā Ḥamzah ʿAynī, may Allāh be pleased with him:]

وراثہ آنکہ مشائخ ازیں جہاں واگزشت وخلیفہ را بجائے خود نگزاشت
وارثے کہ شایاں ایں امر بود بر جادۂ او نشست وخود خلیفہ گرفت

Wirāthah is that a shaykh passes away from this realm without having appointed a khalīfah in his place so an heir of that shaykh who is fit for this position of khilāfah ascends his position and appoints himself as the khalīfah.

أقول كخلافة الأمير معاوية رضي الله تعالى عنه بعد ابن عمه أمير المؤمنين غني قبل تفويض الإمام المجتبى إياه وهذا إن ثبت أنه كان يدعى قبله أنه خليفة وإلا فقد صح أنه رضي الله تعالى عنه ينكر دعوى الخلافة ويقول إني لأعلم أنه يعني علي كرم الله تعالى وجهه أفضل مني وأحق بالأمر ولكن ألستم تعلمون أن عثمان قتل مظلوما وأنا ابن عمه ووليه أطلب دمه رواه يحيى بن سليمان الجعفي شيخ البخاري في كتاب الصفين بسند جيد عن أبي مسلم الخولاني وأما بعد تفويض الإمام المجتبى إياه فلا شك أنه إمام حق وأمير صدق كما بينه العلامة ابن حجر في الصواعق

I say: This is like the *khilāfah* of 'Amīr Muʿāwiyah, may Allāh Almighty be pleased with him, following the son of his uncle, 'Amīr al-Mu'minīn [ʿUthmān] al-Ghanī prior to the entrustment of 'Imām [Ḥasan] al-Mujtabā to him. This is if it is proven that he, may Allāh Almighty be pleased with him, claimed before him that he is the *khalīfah*. Elsewise, it has been authenticated that he, may Allāh Almighty be pleased with him, used to deny the claim of *khilāfah*, and he would say, "I most surely know that he (ʿAlī, may Allāh Almighty ennoble his countenance) is superior to me and more worthy of the affair. However, do you all not know that ʿUthmān was murdered unjustly and that I am the son of his uncle and his representative? I seek the avengement of his blood." This was narrated by Yaḥyā bin Sulaymān al-Juʿfī, the shaykh of *Bukhārī*, in *Kitāb al-Ṣiffīn* with a sound chain of transmission from 'Abū Muslim al-Khawlānī.

As for after the entrustment of 'Imām [Ḥasan] al-Mujtabā to him, then there is no doubt that he is the true 'imām and the righteous leader, as 'Allāmah 'Ibn Ḥajar detailed in al-Ṣawā'iq.[29]

[Continuing the word of Sayyidunā Ḥamzah 'Aynī, may Allāh be pleased with him:]

این نوع را مشائخ منظور نداشته اند واحیانا آں شیخ او را در
باطن امر فرماید روا بود کہ نزد صوفیہ حکم ارواح جائز ست

The mashā'ikh did not accept this type and at times, if the shaykh commands him internally, it is permissible because according to the Ṣūfīs, the command of the souls is valid.

V. 'Uwaysīyah (Spiritual Transmission)

أقول وح يرجع إلى الأويسية كما أن سيدي أبا الحسن الخرقاني
خليفة سيدي أبي يزيد البسطامي قدس الله تعالى أسرارهما ولكن لا
يسلم هذا لكل مدع ما لم نعلم ثقته وعدالته أو يشهد له أهل الباطن
إلى آخر ما أفاده وأجاد قدس الله تعالى سره العزيز

I say: Now we return to the *'Uwaysīyah*. It is just as Sayyidī 'Abū al-Ḥasan al-Kharaqānī is the *khalīfah* of Sayyidī 'Abū Yazīd al-Bisṭāmī, may Allāh Almighty sanctify their secrets. However, this shall not be accepted for just any ordinary claimant – not until we learn of his credibility and honesty, or the *'Ahl al-Bāṭin* (the People of the Inner State) testify for him. From here to the end of what he (Shāh Ḥamzah 'Aynī) has noted and explained well, may Allāh Almighty sanctify his dominant secret.

However, after the validity of *khilāfah 'āmmah*, to practice [as the *khalīfah*] and *'ijmā'* (consensus) is considerable and sufficient.

---

[25] *al-Ṣawā'iq al-Muḥriqah, al-Khātimah fī Bayān 'I`tiqād 'Ahl al-Sunnah*

لأن المعهود عرفا كالمشروط لفظا وما رآه
المسلمون حسنا فهو عند الله حسن

Because that which is understood according to custom is like it has been made a condition verbally,[30] and what the Muslims see as good is good according to Allāh.[31]

In a place such as this, the predominant custom is that the eldest of the children bears the right, and in his presence, another cannot be [the successor]. However, in the case that he is void of the merit or the one appointing the *khalīfah* has issued a considerable bequest of the appointment of someone else entirely or in the partnership and cooperation of someone else alongside him, then to act upon it is certainly inevitable.

Moreover, just as it is acceptable for the one appointing the *khalīfah* to completely deprive his close relative based on a *sharʿī* prudence, he can make someone else his partner or associate based on a prudence. Amongst the reasons of prudence, one reason could be that because one aspect of this blessed position is related to the world and the other to the religion, it is unfathomable that someone possessing only sufficient discernment in one aspect will responsibly tend to all matters. Thus, if the one appointing the *khalīfah*, being someone who is wary of the manners of prudence, sees the discernment of one of his close people towards this way, and that of another to be greater that way, who can prevent the one of intuition and the one who is aware of the results of affairs[32] from appointing the one of more discernment in religion as the *khalīfah* – and with consideration to the other aspect – appointing the one with more discernment of the worldly affairs as his partner and

---

[30] *Radd al-Muḥtār, Kitāb al-Buyūʿ*

[31] *al-Mustadrak li al- Ḥākim: 4465*

[32] *Someone familiar with the outcomes of affairs, the most guided in religion, one who treads the path of righteousness, and from the other standpoint, the most knowledgeable of worldly matters (author)*

making him his supporter? As a result of the joining of views, a composite model can be achieved, and the enduring of all the burdens of this grand position can be manifested in a beautiful manner.

Moreover, the plurality which is impermissible in *'imāmah kubrā* (grand position of being *'imām*) is due to duality[33] being a probable means to great tribulations and horrid battles, as is apparent. It is a well-known parable:

دو بادشاہ درا قیملے نگنجد

Two kings cannot live in a single land.

This *khilāfah*, although very similar to *'imāmah kubrā* – and due to which the excess and plurality which is valid in the first *khilāfah* (*khilāfah 'āmmah*) is unfathomable in this case – it does not share similarity to it in every regard. That is why being from the tribe of *Quraysh* was not made a condition.

And as for the wisdom [behind why duality in this case would be avoided] that this mendicant has mentioned as an example – then, in the case that duality [in *khilāfah khāṣṣah*] does occur, there is no apparent evidence for its invalidation. Whoever claims such, the burden of explanation is upon him. And concerning just the authority of the endowments (*'awqāf*), there is clear evidence of permissibility in the plurality of its supervisors.

However, there is no doubt in the fact that in the tradition of successorship, singularity is the predominant custom. Without a good reason, it should not be contradicted. That being said, the discussion is regarding when the *murshid murabbī*, being someone

---

[33] *For there to be two khalīfahs is a battlefield for the birth of tremendously great tribulations and destructive battles (author)*

who is wary of the manners of prudence and someone who is very great in status, has appointed two successors, there is no way to disregard it. Nevertheless, in the aforementioned scenario, it could be considered that the one of more discernment in the religion is the true successor and the other is the observer and overlooker.

كما أشرنا إليه

As we have indicated towards.

والله تعالى أعلم بالصواب وعنده أم الكتاب وصلى الله تعالى على سيدنا محمد
والآل والأصحاب والخلفاء والنواب والأتباع والأحباب. آمين.

Allāh Almighty is most knowing of accuracy and by Him is 'Umm al-Kitāb. May Allāh Almighty send blessings upon Sayyidunā Muḥammad, the progeny, the companions, the *khulafā'*, the representatives, the followers, and the beloveds. *'Āmīn!*

The Third Question

THE THIRD QUESTION

Oneness of the Shaykh

QUERY EIGHTY-ONE *Shawwāl 23, 1309 H.*

[Sent] With the treatise *Zayb e Ghurfah*, regarding the prohibition of plurality in spiritual allegiance, (*bay'ah*) intending attestation.

Sent by: Janāb Mawlawī Muḥammad 'Abd al-Samī' Ṣāḥib, the *marḥūm* (enveloped in mercy) and *maghfūr* (forgiven), the author of *'Anwār e Sāṭi'ah*

From Meerut

THE ANSWER

بسم الله الرحمن الرحيم

الحمد لله الواحد الأحد المنزه من كل شرك وعدد والصلوة والسلام على النبي الأوحد وآله وصحبه وتابعيهم في الرشد من الأزل إلى أبد الأبد

All praise is for Allāh, the One, the Peerless, the One Far Beyond any Association or Plurality. Blessings and salutations be upon the Matchless Prophet, his progeny, his companions, and their adherents in guidance from the beginning of time to the furthest point of the end of time.

In reality, without a valid, true, and coercive need – in the presence of the *shaykh*, completely avoiding the pledge of allegiance (*bay'ah*) on the hands of another should be considered necessary.

وهو المختار وفيه الخير وفي غيره ضير أيما ضير

That is the chosen position, and in it is virtue. In other than it, there is harm – every type of harm.

Darting eyes and the acts of the undomesticated are a means of deprivation. Allāh, the Lord of all Creations, forbid!

Beware, the Glorious *Qur'ān* explicitly states that it is only best that it be:

وَرَجُلًا سَلَمًا لِّرَجُلٍ

One man belonging to a single man.[34]

[34] *Sūrah al-Zumar: 29*

هَلْ يَسْتَوِيَانِ مَثَلًا الْحَمْدُ لِلَّهِ بَلْ أَكْثَرُهُمْ لَا يَعْلَمُونَ

Are they both equal in comparison? All praise is for Allāh. Rather, the majority of them know not.[35]

The Shaykh is the Focal Point of Attention

Beware, the true *shaykh* is the focal point (*qiblah*) of attention, and to turn away from the *qiblah* is a manifest contradiction to prayer.

Despite having said:

فَأَيْنَمَا تُوَلُّوا فَثَمَّ وَجْهُ اللَّهِ

So, wherever you turn, there is the wajh (pleasure) of Allāh,[36]

It is said to the seekers of *wajh-Allāh*, that:

حَيْثُ مَا كُنتُمْ فَوَلُّوا وُجُوهَكُمْ شَطْرَهُ

Wherever you may be, turn your faces in its (Masjid Ḥarām) direction.[37]

This position is one of *taḥarrī* (exercising personal judgment when unable to access any means which tells the direction of the *qiblah*), the *qiblah* of someone practicing *taḥarrī* is a *qiblah* of *taḥarrī*.

Beware, the people of loyalty consider leaving the door of the masters of the world to go to the court of another to be ungratefulness.

[35] *ibid*

[36] *Sūrah al-Baqarah: 115*

[37] *Sūrah al-Baqarah: 144, 150*

سر اینجا سجده اینجا بندگی اینجا قرار اینجا

The head is at this place, the prostration is at this place,
the servanthood is at this place, solace is at this place.

Thus, what is the match of the favors of the *dunyā* in comparison to those of the honorable *shaykh*? How strange is he who makes the claim of love and sincerity for the *shaykh* yet, in his presence, sings the praise of this person or that person.

چو دل با دلبری آرام گیرد
زوصل دیگرے کے کام گیرد

When the heart finds solace with one beloved,
How will it attain its desire by meeting with another?

نہی صد دستہ ریحاں پیش بلبل
نخواہد خاطرش جز نگہت گل

Place a hundred bundles of basil before the nightingale,
But its heart shall not desire except the fragrance of the flower.

Beware, the *fayḍ* (the spiritual abundance of bounties) of the *shaykh* is *mann* and *salwā*, and it will lead to a poor outcome to say:

لَن نَّصْبِرَ عَلَى طَعَامٍ وَاحِدٍ

We will never be enduring of one food! [38]

فلا تكن إسرائيليا وكن محمديا يأتيك رزقك بكرة وعشيا

Thus, do not be an Israelite. Be Muḥammadan.
Your provision shall come to you day and night.

[38] *Sūrah al-Baqarah: 61*

The Station of the Shaykh

Beware, the father is the father of the physical body, and the *shaykh* is the father of the heart. The master is the emancipator of the physical body, and the *shaykh* emancipates the pure soul. To reprimand the people of desire, this *ḥadīth* is sufficient: He who tells his father to be someone other than his father, or he who takes another as a master in the presence of his master, upon him is the curse of Allāh, the Angels, and of all people. Allāh Almighty will not accept his *farḍ* (obligatory acts of worship), nor *nafl* (voluntary acts of worship).

الأئمة الخمسة عن أمير المؤمنين علي كرم الله تعالى وجهه عن النبي
صلى الله تعالى عليه وسلم من ادعى إلى غير أبيه أو انتمى إلى غير مواليه
فعليه لعنة الله والملائكة والناس أجمعين لا يقبل الله منه صرفا ولا عدلا

The five 'imāms narrate from 'Amīr al-Mu'minīn 'Alī, may Allāh Almighty ennoble his countenance, [and he] from the Prophet , may Allāh send blessings and salutations upon him, "Whoever claims [connection] to other than his own father, or takes someone other than his master as a master, upon him is the curse of Allāh, the Angels, and the people in totality. Allāh does not accept his farḍ, nor nafl."[39]

Those who have committed such acts out of jest, do they not fear that they may receive, by way of *qiyās jalī* (obvious analogy), the horrid threat of this authentic *ḥadīth*?

Beware, those who have always been fortunate themselves, despite the command of the *shaykh*, refused to abandon the *shaykh*. And what was the reality of this abandonment? It was leaving a spring to go to an overflowing ocean. Yet, despite it all,

[39] *Ṣaḥīḥ Muslim: 1370a*

they did not tolerate forsaking the court of the *shaykh*, and this etiquette of theirs was taken a liking to by the beloveds of Allāh.

A Story of Shaykh 'Alī bin Haytī's Disciple

His Luminous Eminence, the Master of the Noble *'Awliyā'*, the *'Imām* of the Grand Gnostics, the Honorable Sayyidunā Ghawth 'A`ẓam, may Allāh be pleased with him, arrived at the place of the Honorable Sayyidī 'Alī bin Haytī, may his magnificent secret be sanctified. The Honorable 'Alī bin Haytī commanded his distinguished disciple and specified successor, Sayyidī 'Abū al-Ḥasan 'Alī Jawsaqī, may the mercy of Allāh Almighty be upon him, that he take on the responsibility of serving the Honorable Ghawth, may Allāh be pleased with him, and he had informed him prior that, "I am of the slaves of His Luminous Eminence, Ghawth 'A`ẓam, may Allāh be pleased with him."

Upon hearing this much from the *shaykh*, Sayyidī 'Abū al-Ḥasan, may his secret be sanctified, began to weep and did not wish, in any way, to forsake the court of the *shaykh*. Upon seeing him crying, His Eminence, the *Ghawth* (succor) of the *'Awliyā'*, may Allāh be pleased with him, said:

ما يحب إلا الثدي الذي رضع منه

He does not prefer a bosom save the
one from which he has been suckled.

And he commanded him to remain in the service of his *shaykh*.

أخرج سيدي الإمام نور الدين أبو الحسن علي بن يوسف اللخمي
قدس سره في كتابه بهجة الأسرار ومعدن الأنوار بسند صحيح
عن سيدي أبي حفص عمر البزار قدس الله تعالى سره

Related by Sayyidī 'Imām Nūr al-Dīn 'Abū al-Ḥasan 'Alī bin Yūsuf al-Lakhmī, may his secret be sanctified, in his book, Bahjah al-'Asrār wa Ma'din al-'Anwār [40]*, with a ṣaḥīḥ (authentic) chain of transmission from 'Abū Ḥafṣ 'Umar al-Bazzār, may Allāh Almighty sanctify his secret.*

The Gnostic of Allāh, the Most Sublime '*Imām*, Sayyidī 'Abd al-Wahhāb al-Sha'rānī, may his divine secret be sanctified, states in *Mīzān al-Sharī'ah al-Kubrā*:

سمعت سيدي عليا الخواص رحمه الله يقول إنما امر علماء الشريعة الطالب بالتزام مذهب معين وعلماء الحقيقة المريد بالتزام شيخ واحد

I heard Sayyidī 'Alī al-Khawwāṣ, may Allāh envelope him in mercy, saying, "Verily, the scholars of the sharī'ah have commanded the student the commitment of a specified madh-hab, and the scholars of spirituality [have commanded] the disciple the commitment to one shaykh." [41]

Thereafter, the aforementioned saint, may his beneficial secret be sanctified, clarified this matter with an explicit example. 'Imām 'Allāmah 'Abdarī Makkī, alias 'Ibn al-Ḥājj, may the mercy of Allāh Almighty be upon him, says in the blessed *Madkhal*:

المريد يعظم شيخه ويؤثره على غيره ممن هو في وقته لأن النبي صلى الله تعالى عليه وسلم يقول من رزق في شيء فليلزمه إلى آخر ما أفاد وأجاد هذا مختصر

The disciple reveres his shaykh and gives him preference over others who share his era because the Prophet, may Allāh send blessings and salutations upon him, says, "Whoever is granted provision in anything, he should adhere to it." [42] *(to the end of what he noted and said beautifully – this is a summary)*

---

[40] *Bahjah al-'Asrār, Dhikr 'Abū al-Ḥasan 'Alī al-Jawsaqī*

[41] *al-Mīzān al-Kubrā, Faṣl fa 'in Qulta fa 'idhā Infakka Qalb al-Walī 'an al-Taqlīd*

[42] *al-Madkhal li 'Ibn al-Ḥājj, Ḥaqīqah 'Akhdh al-'Ahd*

Also, in this is:

إن المريد له اتساع في حسن الظن بهم وفي ارتباطه على شخص واحد يعول عليه في أموره ويحذر من تقضي أوقاته لغير فائدة

Verily, there is abundance for the disciple in thinking positively of them (all mashā'ikh) and in the commitment to a single shaykh upon whom he relies in his affairs, and he shall be wary of passing his time to no benefit.[43]

Note: This *ḥadīth* that the aforementioned *'imām* related as *mu'ḍal*[44] is a sound *ḥadīth*.

أخرجه البيهقي في شعب الإيمان بسند حسن عن أنس رضي الله تعالى عنه وهو عند ابن ماجه من حديثه ومن حديث أم المؤمنين الصديقة رضي الله تعالى عنهما عن النبي صلى الله تعالى عليه وسلم بلفظ من بورك له في شيء فليلزمه

Bayhaqī related it in Shu'ab al-'Īmān[45] *with a sound chain of transmission from 'Anas, may Allāh Almighty be pleased with him. According to 'Ibn Mājah, it is from his ḥadīth and also from the ḥadīth of 'Umm al-Mu'minīn al-Ṣiddīqah, may Allāh Almighty be pleased with them both, [narrating] from the Prophet, may Allāh Almighty send blessings and salutations upon him, in the wording, "Whoever is granted blessing in anything, he should adhere to it."* [46]

This astonishing derivation from it is exquisite and magnificent.

---

[43] *al-Madkhal li 'Ibn al-Ḥājj, Faṣl fī Dukhūl al-Murīd al-Khalwah*

[44] *Mu'ḍal: a report in whose chain of transmission two or more consecutive narrators are omitted (translator)*

[45] *Shu'ab al-'Īmān: 1241*

[46] *al-'Asrār al-Ma'rūfah, with reference to Sunan 'Ibn Mājah: 887*

والحمد لله على ما رزق ومن والصلوة والسلام على رسوله الأمن وآله وصحبه
وكل من آمن والله تعالى أعلم وعلمه جل مجده أتم وحكمه عز شأنه أحكم

All praise is for Allāh upon what He provided and granted as a favor. Blessings and salutations be upon His Messenger, the most granting of favors, upon his progeny, companions, and all those who believed. ***Allāh Almighty knows best, and His knowledge – majestic is His glory – is most perfect, and His rule – sublime is His grandeur – is most just.***

The Fourth Question

THE FOURTH QUESTION

He Who Has no Shaykh

QUERY EIGHTY-TWO *Shawwāl 15, 1317 H.*

What do the scholars of the religion say in the following matter:

Zayd says and writes in his book:

من لا شيخ له في الدنيا فشيخ له شيطان في الآخرة

He who has no shaykh in the dunyā, his shaykh is Shayṭān in the hereafter

In other words, on the Day of Judgment, he will be resurrected amongst the congregation of *Shayṭān*.

His Eminence, may Allāh send blessings and salutations upon him, states:

الشيخ في قومه كالنبي في الأمة

The shaykh, amongst his people, is
comparable to a prophet amongst his nation.[47]

In other words, just as the nation (*'ummah*) is guided by a prophet, the disciple is guided by the *shaykh* or *murshid*. The nation to which a prophet has not come is astray and similarly, the one without a *shaykh* is misguided.

The Honorable Shaykh al-Mashā'ikh Niẓām al-Dīn 'Awliyā', Maḥbūb 'Ilāhī (a title of the *shaykh* which means: the beloved of Allāh), may Allāh be pleased with him, has written in *Rāḥat al-Qulūb*, "The individual not in the boundaries of the shirttail[48] of the *'Awliyā'* of Allāh, or in other words has no *shaykh*, is outside the folds of *'Islām* such that his slavery [to Allāh] is not accepted. His prayer and fasting are akin to a lantern without fuel."

Some of the noble *ṣūfīs* have said that the *salām* of the *shaykh*-less shall be responded to with "*hadāka Allāh* (may Allāh guide you)," and the one who responds with "*'alayka* (upon you)," purposely to the *shaykh*-less has sided with the *Shayṭān*. [As seen in the] Stanza:

---

[47] *al-Maqāṣid al-Ḥasanah: 609*

[48] *This literally refers to the lower portion of the upper garment which hangs below the waist, also called dāman in the Urdu language. This is figurative speech which means to be associated with something. (translator)*

اگر بے پیر کارے پیش گیرد
بلاکی را ز بہر خویش گیرد

If he takes on any task without a shaykh,
It is destruction he has taken on for himself!

بنا گرو کی مالا جپنا جنم اکارت جائے

Constant recitation of litanies without a guide is equivalent to destruction of life.

Furthermore, Bakr says, "I have not pledged allegiance to any individual, I pray *ṣalāh*, I fast, I deem true the rulings of the blessed *sharīʿah*, the Glorious Word [of Allāh], and that which the scholars of the religion state. However, I am not the disciple of any ascetic *shaykh* and nor do I say that to be a disciple is wrongful."

Thence, in this scenario, as a result of Zayd's word, no form of worship performed by Bakr will be accepted in the court of al-Bārī Almighty; all forms of worship performed by Bakr without having become a disciple have gone in vain. [To say,] "*Salām ʿAlayka*" to Bakr would thus be impermissible, Bakr would have left the folds of *ʿIslām* and would be resurrected in the congregation of *shayāṭīn* (pl. of *Shayṭān*).

Thereupon, what is Bakr to do in this situation?

THE ANSWER

The *shaykh*, i.e., the one who shows the way to, or is a guide to, or one who leads to the path of Allāh, is of two types:

1. *'Āmm (General)*: The guide is the Word of Allāh, the word of the Messenger, the word of the *'imāms* of the *sharī'ah* and *ṭarīqah* (spirituality), and the word of the scholars of the outward and inward states in this uninterrupted chain that the guide of the laymen is the word of the scholars, the guide of the scholars is the word of the *'imāms*, the guide of the *'imāms* is the word of the Messenger, and the guide of the Messenger is the Word of Allāh.

2. *Khāṣṣ (Specific)*: That Zayd pledges allegiance on the hands of a specific servant of Allāh who is a guide, is guided, worthy of leadership and guidance, and someone who simultaneously possesses all requirements of *bay'ah* (spiritual allegiance), and that he (Zayd) remains adherent to his guidance which is in accordance with the *sharī'ah* and the *ṭarīqah* in his talks, walks, actions, and inactions.

A guiding *shaykh* in the first meaning is incumbent upon all. And such a *shaykh*-less individual (in the first meaning of *shaykh*) is far from *'Islām*. His worship is in vain and rejected. To precede in *salām* to him is prohibited and forbidden. On the Day of Judgment, he will be resurrected in the congregation of *Shayṭān*. Allāh Almighty states

يَوْمَ نَدْعُوا كُلَّ أُنَاسٍ بِإِمَامِهِمْ

On that day that We summon every community with their leader.[49]

[49] *Sūrah al-'Isrā'*: 71

When this individual did not take the *'imāms* of guidance as his guide, he became a disciple of the *'imām* of misguidance, i.e., the accursed *Shayṭān*. Certainly, on the Day of Judgment, he will rise in his congregation, Allāh Almighty forbid.

However, amongst those who proclaim the *shahādah*, this category of *shaykh*-less individuals can be split into four subcategories:

I. The *kāfir* (disbeliever) who outright fail to believe in the *Qur'ān* and *Ḥadīth*, such as the Naturalists (*Necharī*) who explicitly say for the *'aḥādīth* to be rejected and futile and they reject the definite and explicit (*qaṭ'ī*) meanings of the *Qur'ān* to distort them into tales and fables from their own hearts. May Allāh curse them severely.

II. The *Ghayr-muqallids* (non-*muqallids*) who, on the surface, believe in the *Qur'ān* and *Ḥadith* but believe for the statements of the *'imāms* of the religion and the carriers of the mighty *sharī'ah* to be inconsiderable. They seek direct connection to Allāh and the Messenger after breaking the chain of allegiance.

وَسَيَعْلَمُ الَّذِينَ ظَلَمُوا أَيَّ مُنْقَلَبٍ يَنْقَلِبُونَ

And soon those who oppress shall learn what place of return they shall return to.[50]

III. The *Muqallid Wahhābīs* who, on the surface, exercise nominal *taqlīd* of the *'imāms* in the *furū'* matters of jurisprudence (*fiqh*), but in terms of *'uṣūl* and creed, they tread a path contrary to that of the *Sawād 'A'ẓam* (the Greater Group). They are also enraged at the mention of the stations, ranks, and supremacy of the noble *'awliyā'*.

[50] *Sūrah al-Shu'arā': 227*

IV. Similar are all misguided sects, the deluded, the astray, the *Rawāfiḍ* (pl. of *Rāfiḍī*), the *Khawārij* (pl. of *Khārijī*), the *Muʿtazilah*, the *Qadarīyah*, the *Jabarīyah*, etc., may Allāh devastate them, as they, abandoning the path of guidance, took their desire as an ʿ*imām* and thus connected their chain of allegiance to the accursed *Shayṭān*. Allāh Almighty says:

أَفَرَأَيْتَ مَنِ اتَّخَذَ إِلَٰهَهُ هَوَاهُ

Do you see the one who takes his desire as his deity?[51]

In summary, the comprehensive word is that the people of desire, i.e., all adversaries of the ʿ*Ahl al-Sunnah*, are the ones who are without a true *shaykh* in this meaning and are truly deserving of all such rulings.

قَاتَلَهُمُ اللَّهُ أَنَّىٰ يُؤْفَكُونَ

Allāh destroy them, to where do they divert?[52]

The *Sunnī* of proper creed who believes in the ʿ*imāms* of guidance, considers necessary the *taqlīd* of the ʿ*imāms*, is a true lover of the noble ʿ*awliyā*ʾ, and is steadfast in all beliefs on the path of truth, is certainly not *shaykh*-less. All four of those pure guides, i.e., the Word of Allāh and the Messenger, the ʿ*imāms*, and the scholars of the outward and inward states, are his *shaykh*. Rather, if he is upon this very state, then similar to thousands of the Muslims of the ʿ*Ahl al-Sunnah*, his hand is in the hand of the pure *sharīʿah* although, on the surface, he has not been honored by placing his hand in the blessed hand of a particular servant of Allāh.

---

[51] *Sūrah al-Jāthiyah: 23*

[52] *Sūrah al-Tawbah: 30*

عهد مابالب شیریں دہناں بست خدائے
ماہمہ بندہ وایں قوم خداوند انند

Allāh has tied our era to the people of sweet mouths,
We are all servants, and those people are masters.

The individual who seeks to tread the path of *sulūk* (spiritual wayfaring) requires even the *shaykh* and guide (*murshid*) in the second meaning (*khāṣṣ*). This is not a path man can tread on basis of his own whim or by studying books; each man faces new adversities therein according to everyone's own capability and state which cannot be resolved except by the attention of a particular and perfect guide.

However, to apply such harsh rulings upon abandoning this is simply absurd, a futile lie, explicit oppression, and a manifest slander against the religion of Allāh. Firstly, those who journey this path are very little and those who do desire this, in this era of darkness, sinisterness, concealment of the majority of the people of *wilāyah*, the crowd of the world, and seekers of boastful character, it is difficult for the perfect (*kāmil*) *shaykh* to be accessible at all times.

اے بسا ابلیس آدم روے ہست
پس بہر دستے نباید دادوست

How many a time, the devil appears in form of man,
Thence, the hand shall not be submitted into just any hand!

Thousands of scholars and pious people have passed whose connection in this particular method of *bay'ah* is not proven apparently. Can they, Allāh forbid, be deemed subject to these harsh rulings? And those who did become connected, did they become connected as soon as they acquired the faculty of reason? Not at all! Rather, a plethora of them did at the time they had reached the lofty rank of leadership (*'imāmah*) in outward knowledge. Were they deserving, Allāh forbid, of such rulings until that time? This is sheer, clear, and manifest ignorance – *wa al-ʿayādhu bi-Allāh taʿālā* (refuge is with Allāh Almighty)!

The first *ḥadīth* Zayd presented, there is no sign of it in the word of the Messenger, may Allāh send blessings and salutations upon him, however it is the statement of the *ʿawliyā*'. The second *ḥadīth*:

الشيخ في قومه كالنبي في أمته

The shaykh, amongst his people, is comparable to a prophet amongst his nation.[53]

– which ʿIbn Ḥibbān, in *Kitāb al-Ḍuʿafā*', and Daylamī, in *Musnad al-Firdaws*, narrated from the Honorable ʿAbū Rāfiʿ, may Allāh be pleased with him, that the Messenger of Allāh, may Allāh send blessings and salutations upon him, said such. Although ʿImām ʿIbn Ḥajar ʿAsqalānī, and ʿIbn Taymīyah prior to him, deemed it a fabrication *(mawḍūʿ)*, and ʿImām Sakhāwī called it baseless *(bāṭil)*, it is apparent from the methodology of the sublime ʿImām Jalāl Suyūṭī that it is only *ḍaʿīf* (weak), and not baseless and fabricated. He presented this *ḥadīth* in two ways in *Jāmiʿ Ṣaghīr*:

حيث قال الشيخ في أهله كالنبي في أمته والخليلي في مشيخته وابن النجار عن أبي رافع
الشيخ في بيته كالنبي في قومه حب في الضعفاء والشيرازي في الألقاب عن ابن عمر

Such that he said, "'The shaykh, amongst his people, is like the prophet amongst his nation' and Khalīlī in his Mashīkhah and ʿIbn al-Najjār [narrated] from ʿAbū Rāfiʿ[54]*. 'The shaykh, in his abode, is like the prophet, in his community,' ʿIbn Ḥibbān [narrated it] in al-Ḍuʿafā', Shīrāzī in al-ʿAlqāb from ʿIbn ʿUmar.*[55]"

[53] *al-Maqāṣid al-Ḥasanah: 609*

[54] *al-Jāmiʿ al-Ṣaghīr: 4969*

[55] *al-Jāmiʿ al-Ṣaghīr: 4970*

Moreover, he promised in the preface (khuṭbah) of the book that, "I will not present any fabrication in this book."

حيث قال تركت القشر وأخذت اللباب وصنته عما تفرد به وضاع أو كذاب

Such that he said, "I abandoned the skin and took the flesh. I safeguarded it from that which any fabricator or liar has reported solitarily."[56]

However, only this much is proven from this that obedience to the guides of the path of Allāh is necessary. What discussion is in this? Sufficient for this is the noble verse itself:

أَطِيعُوا اللهَ وَأَطِيعُوا الرَّسُولَ وَأُولِي الْأَمْرِ مِنكُمْ

Obey Allāh and obey the Messenger and those of authority from you.[57]

Upon the most correct and preferable opinion, by *'ūlu al-'amr* (those of authority), the scholars of the religion are intended, as it is inclusive of the scholars of the *sharī'ah* and the scholars of *ṭarīqah* both. To derive a meaning beyond this, that, "Whoever does not apparently pledge allegiance on the hands of someone is misguided," is certainly not the fruit of the *ḥadīth*. This is slander and accusation or ignorance and foolishness. *Wa al-'ayādhu bi-Allāh ta'ālā* (refuge is with Allāh Almighty)!

However, it has been stated regarding the grand *bay'ah* and *'imāmah ('imāmah kubrā)* in an authentic *ḥadīth*:

من خلع يدا من طاعة لقي الله يوم القيامة لا حجة
له ومن مات وليس في عنقه بيعة مات ميتة جاهلية

Whoever restrains a hand from obedience shall meet Allāh on the Day of Judgment without having any argument, and whoever dies and is not bound by the pledge of allegiance, he has died a death of the days of ignorance (Jāhilīyah).[58]

---

[56] *al-Jāmi' al-Ṣaghīr, Khuṭbah al-Mu'allif*

[57] *Sūrah al-Nisā': 59*

[58] *Ṣaḥīḥ Muslim: 1851a*

'Imām Muslim narrated it from 'Abd Allāh bin 'Umar, may Allāh be pleased with them.

That too in the case that the *'imām* is present and accessible as is apparent, and otherwise:

لَا يُكَلِّفُ اللّٰهُ نَفْسًا إِلَّا وُسْعَهَا

Allāh does not burden a soul except to its capacity.[59]

Allāh Almighty knows best.

[59] *Sūrah al-Baqarah: 286*

The Fifth Question

THE FIFTH QUESTION

Rulings Concerning the Successor

QUERY EIGHTY-THREE *Shawwāl 17, 1317 H.*

From Kichhauchha Sharīf, Fayḍābād District

Sent by: The Honorable Sayyid Shāh 'Abū al-Maḥmūd Mawlānā Mawlawī 'Aḥmad 'Ashraf Miyāñ Ṣāḥib 'Ashrafī, may his glory be prolonged

What do the sublime scholars and the noble *mashā'ikh* (pl. of *shaykh*) say in the following matter?

The time of five hundred years has passed since Zayd and 'Amr, both full brothers, were each separately granted two *khirqahs* (an initiatory cloak granted to successors in the spiritual chains) by one guide *(murshid)*, i.e., their noble father, and thus attained *khilāfah* and successorship. Zayd, the elder son, has continuously, on the day of the *murshid's 'urs* (death anniversary), specifically donned the *khirqah* granted by the *shaykh* in the shrine of the *shaykh* and performed the *fātiḥah* of the *'urs* according to the tradition of the *mashā'ikh*. In this manner, for eight generations in the progeny of Zayd, the household *khilāfah* and the [ceremony of] *khirqah-poshī* (a ceremony wherein the next successor of the spiritual chain is granted the cloak) in the sense of successorship remained established.

The final successor of the eighth generation, Bakr, passed away leaving behind his wife, Hindah, and his brother and particular *khalīfah (khalīfah khāṣṣ)*, Khālid. Following the demise of her husband, Hindah went to her pre-marital home taking along the aforementioned *khirqah*. The chain of allegiance and the household *khilāfah* has continued for about one hundred years, but due to the stated reason, the *khirqah-poshī* has not been able to take place in this time period. In the progeny of ʿAmr, the younger son, the *khirqah-poshī* would take place one day prior to the *ʿurs* until the ninth generation as the *khirqa-poshī* on the day of the *ʿurs* itself would take place in the progeny of the elder son.

When the tradition could not be fulfilled in the era of Khālid due to the absence of the *khirqah*, Rashīd, the ninth successor of ʿAmr and the contemporary of Khālid, held the *khirqah-poshī* on both days. At present, in the chain of ʿAmr is Ḥāmid, and in the offspring of Zayd is Maḥmūd, who apart from the allegiance and *khilāfah*, became a senior of the household and also took back the *khirqah* and completely restored the lost tradition once again. Now, Ḥāmid is in disagreement concerning his deserving the *khirqah-poshī*. The household *khilafah* upuntil the *shaykh* of the *shaykh* of Maḥmūd (Maḥmūd's grand-shaykh) is accepted by many of the dear ones of the family members and is well-known amongst them. Some seniors of the family members have also recorded this in their published treatises. The *shaykh* of Maḥmūd, who was from the credible and just, was granted a written and signed certificate of *khilāfah* from his *shaykh* from his own blessed pen which his own son a nd many others know of. They continued this chain for much time; the people continued to become disciples of his, then of Maḥmūd, then of the *khulafā'* of Maḥmūd. The seniors of the scholars and *mashā'ikh* of the era accepted Maḥmūd as the *khalīfah* and successor of the household and placed their seals of approval on this. Rather, the *shaykh* of the *shaykh* of Maḥmūd himself wrote "*Sajjādah-nashīn* (successor)" in the titles alongside the name of Maḥmūd in a signed letter.

In this scenario, will this chain of *khilāfah* and successorship be established and accepted, or will it not be accepted on the basis of the denial of some who dispute it? Moreover, after the tradition of *khirqah-poshī* being practiced continuously for four hundred years in the family of Maḥmūd, then being discontinued for approximately one hundred years due to the aforementioned reason, and by the *khirqah-poshī* being held on both days by Ḥāmid's family, has the right of Maḥmūd been terminated, or can he reinstate this tradition? Does Ḥāmid bear the right to objection and opposition of the *khirqah-poshī* of Maḥmūd on the day of the *'urs*, specifically in the confines of the shrine on basis of the previously stated reasons, or not?

Explain and be rewarded!

THE ANSWER

In the scenario regarding which the question was asked, the household *khilāfah* and successorship of Maḥmūd is certainly established and accepted, and the denial of those who dispute it will not be paid any heed. In *sharʿī* and rational terms, there are two methods to establish such affairs:

I. *ʿIttiṣāl al-Sanad* (continuity in the chain)
II. Popularity

It is manifest from the details of the question that Maḥmūd possesses both modes of establishment in a well-established manner. Thus, the negation of the negator is certainly unheeded and baseless.

It is [stated] in *Fatḥ al-Qadīr, al-Baḥr al-Rāʾiq, al-Nahr al-Fāʾiq, Minaḥ al-Ghaffār,* and *Radd al-Muḥtār:*

طريق نقله لذلك عن المجتهد أحد أمرين إما أن يكون له سند فيه أو يأخذه من كتاب معروف تداولته الأيدي نحو كتب محمد بن الحسن ونحوها من التصانيف المشهورة للمجتهدين لأنه بمنزلة الخبر المتواتر المشهور هكذا ذكر الرازي

The method of its reporting for that from the mujtahid is one of two affairs: either his chain of transmission be in it or that he takes it from a renowned book which the hands circulate, the like of the books of Muḥammad bin al-Ḥasan and its likes from the renowned written works of the mujtahids as it is in the position of a mass-transmitted and renowned report. Such has been mentioned by Rāzī.[60]

When, by explicit mention of the noble *ʿimāms* of the religion of Allāh, the rulings of *ḥalāl* and *ḥarām,* the *fatāwā* and judicial verdicts relating to blood and prohibitions, the presence of

[60] *Radd al-Muḥtār, Kitāb al-Qaḍāʾ, referencing al-Fatḥ, al-Baḥr, and al-Minaḥ*

merely one of the two methods, chain of transmission and popularity, is sufficient and upon whose basis even *ḥudūd* and *qiṣāṣ* (fixed legal penalties) can be enforced, then in the matter of successorship, to not consider even their joined presence as sufficient is completely far from justice.

The state of the chain of transmission is such that when Zayd, whose statement is being heard, narrates a *ḥadīth* or law of jurisprudence from his *shaykh* wherein there is not even explicit mention of [directly] hearing – then even in that case, according to 'Imām Bukhārī and a few other *'imāms*, just the *shaykh* and the disciple meeting at any time is sufficient for accepting [the report]. And according to 'Imām Muslim and the majority of the seniors, this is not required and mere contemporaneity, i.e., the two sharing an era and the possibility of meeting, is sufficient on its own. According to our scholars, this very position is accurate and not that he say, "I heard...," or, "...informed me...," or, "... related the *ḥadīth* to me...," as now, without having met the aforementioned condition, it is accepted, and to consider necessary to ask of the person of the chain [to produce] a witness upon the claim of [direct] hearing is, by consensus of the *'imāms*, erroneous and contemptible.

In the preface of his *Ṣaḥīḥ*, 'Imām Muslim writes:

زعم القائل الذي افتتحنا الكلام على الحكاية عن قوله أن كل إسناد فيه فلان عن فلان وقد أحاط العلم بأنهما كانا في عصر واحد وجائز أن يكون سمعه منه غير أنه لم نجد في الروايات أنهما التقيا لم يكن حجة وهذا القول مخترع مستحدث والمتفق عليه بين أهل العلم قديما وحديثا أن الرواية ثابتة والحجة بها لازمة إلا أن تكون هناك دلالة بينة أن الراوي لم يلق من روى عنه اهـ ملخصا

The speaker – from whose statement is the story which we commenced the discussion upon – assumes that every chain of transmission wherein it is "so-and-so [narrating] from so-and-so," while it is well-established that both of them (the narrator and the listener) were present in a single era and it is possible that he had heard from him, yet, since we do not find in the reports that they both met, will not be [admissible] evidence. This position is unclassical – an innovation. That which is agreed upon amongst the men of knowledge, the classical and the contemporary, is that the narration is established and necessarily admissible as evidence, unless there is clear evidence that the narrator has not met who he narrates from.[61]

It is in *Sharḥ* 'Imām Nawawī:

هذا الذي صار إليه مسلم قد أنكره المحققون وقالوا هذا ضعيف والذي رده هو
المختار الصحيح الذي عليه أئمة الفن علي بن المديني والبخاري وغيرهما

This is what Muslim has demonstrated inclination towards. The researchers have disputed it, and they say it is weak. That which he has rejected is the selected [position] and authentic, that which the 'imāms of the subject, 'Alī bin al-Madīnī, Bukhārī, and others are upon.[62]

It is in *Fatḥ al-Qadīr*, the Chapter of *Witr*:

ما نقل عن البخاري من أنه أعله بقوله لا يعرف سماع بعض هؤلاء من
بعض فبناء على اشتراطه العلم باللقي والصحيح الاكتفاء بإمكان اللقي

What has been reported from Bukhārī, that he would discredit it by saying, "the listening of some of them from others is unknown," is upon the basis of him making the knowledge of the meeting a condition. And what is accurate is sufficiency by the possibility of the meeting.[63]

Moreover, in *Kitāb al-Zakāh, Faṣl fī al-Baqar*, he said:

قول الجمهور الاكتفاء بالمعاصرة ما لم يعلم عدم اللقاء وشرط البخاري
وابن المديني العلم باجتماعهما ولو مرة والحق خلافه اه ملتقطا

---

[61] *Ṣaḥīḥ Muslim, Muqaddimah al-Kitāb*

[62] *Sharḥ Ṣaḥīḥ Muslim li al-Nawawī, Muqaddimah al-Kitāb*

[63] *Fatḥ al-Qadīr, Kitāb al-Ṣalāh, Bāb al-Witr*

The position of the majority is sufficiency with contemporaneity as long as the absence of a meeting is not known. The condition of Bukhārī and 'Ibn al-Madīnī is to know of their meeting, be it once. The truth is contrary to it.[64]

The *khilāfah* and successorship of Zayd and `Amr aside, even the companionship of His Luminous Eminence, may Allāh send blessings and salutations upon him – whose impact surpasses actions and extends to creed, as to revere and love the *Ṣaḥābah* is necessary in the school of the *'Ahl al-Sunnah,* and, Allāh forbid, to disrespect and belittle them is misguidance and it is to be misled – the research scholars say regarding it that for a credible and just person to report on their own behalf that, "I have attained the honor of the companionship of al-Muṣṭafā, may Allāh send blessings and salutations upon him," is sufficient even if his being a companion is not proven at all by any other means, so long as he was present in such a time wherein him attaining this blessing is fathomable.

'Imām 'Ibn Ḥajar `Asqalānī states in *'Iṣābah fī Tamyīz al-Ṣaḥābah:*

الفصل الثاني في الطريق إلى معرفة كون الشخص صحابيا وذلك بأشياء أولها أن يثبت بطريق التواتر أنه صحابي ثم بالاستفاضة والشهرة ثم بأن يروي عن أحد من الصحابة أن فلانا له صحبة مثلا وكذا عن آحاد التابعين بناء على قبول التزكية من واحد وهو الراجح ثم بأن يقول هو إذا كان ثابت العدالة والمعاصرة أنا صحابي

The Second Section regarding the way to recognize an individual as being a ṣaḥābī: That is by several methods: the first of them is that it be established by way of mass-transmission (tawātur) that he is a ṣaḥābī, then by abundant circulation and popularity [of a report], then that it be narrated from any one of the Ṣaḥābah that "so-and-so acquired companionship," for example.

---

[64] *Fatḥ al-Qadīr, Kitāb al-Zakāh, Faṣl fī al-Baqar*

Likewise, is if it is [narrated] from any individual of the Tābi'ūn based upon the [concept of] establishing credibility from one [reporter], and that is the preferable [position]. Then, that he says, while his honesty and contemporaneity are established that, "I am a ṣaḥābī."[65]

It is in *Musallam al-Thubūt:*

إخبار العدل عن نفسه بأنه صحابي إذا كان معاصرا لا كالرتن ليس كتعديله نفسه

The informing of a credible person on his own behalf that he is a ṣaḥābī, in the case that he is a contemporary [of the Prophet, upon him be blessings and salutations] – unlike Ratan [al-Hindī] – is not akin to self-attestation of credibility.[66]

There are numerous *Ṣaḥābah* whose narrations have been related by the *'imāms* of *Ḥadīth*, the classical and the contemporary, in their *Ṣiḥāḥ*, *Masānīd*, *Sunan*, and *Ma'ājim*. They neither had any statement of the Prophet, may Allāh send blessings and salutations upon him, that, "So-and-so was honored by presence in my court of universal refuge," nor was any testimony taken upon this from them, and nor was the attestation of other *Ṣaḥābah* demanded from them. The statement of those credible individuals alone that, "I heard the Messenger of Allāh, may Allāh send blessings and salutations upon him," or "I saw the Messenger of Allāh, may Allāh send blessings and salutations upon him," or "I witnessed the Messenger of Allāh, may Allāh send blessings and salutations upon him," was heard and was accepted.

كما أفاده الإمام أبو عمر بن عبد البر في الاستيعاب وأقره عليه حافظ الشأن

As 'Imām 'Abū 'Umar bin 'Abd al-Barr has noted in *al-'Istī'āb*, and Ḥāfiz al-Sha'n ('Ibn Ḥajar) has attested to it.

---

[65] *al-'Iṣābah fī Tamyīz al-Ṣaḥābah, Khuṭbah al-Kitāb, al-Faṣl al-Thānī*

[66] *Musallam al-Thubūt, al-'Aṣl al-Thānī al-Sunnah, Mas'alah 'Ikhbār al-'Adl 'an Nafsihī*

Popularity (a report being well-known, *shuhrah)* is that by which, let alone the relation of *khilāfah,* the relation of lineage, which is the basis for hundreds of rulings concerning permissibility, prohibition, rights, and entitlement, is even established lawfully (by standards of the *sharī'ah),* rationally, by consensus, by traditional custom, and in every way.

We testify that Sayyidunā Ṣiddīq 'Akbar, may Allāh be pleased with him, is the pure son of the Honorable 'Abū Quḥāfah, may Allāh be pleased with him, and that 'Imām Zayn al-'Ābidīn is the purified son of the Honorable Sayyidunā 'Imām Ḥusayn, may Allāh be pleased with them. Apart from popularity [of the information], what evidence do we possess for this?

It is in *Fatāwā Khulāṣah:*

أما النسب فصورته إذا سمع من إنسان أن فلانا ابن فلان الفلاني وسعه أن
يشهد بذلك وإن لم يعاين الولادة على فراشه أ لا يرى أنا نشهد أن أبا بكر
الصديق رضي الله تعالى عنه ابن أبي قحافة وما رأينا أبا قحافة رضي الله تعالى عنه

As for lineage, its state is that when it is heard from any person that so-and-so is the son of so-and-so from so-and-so place, it permits him to testify by that even if he did not eyewitness the birth on his bed. Does one not see that we testify that 'Abū Bakr al-Ṣiddīq, may Allāh Almighty be pleased with him, is the son of 'Abū Quḥāfah although we have not seen 'Abū Quḥāfah, may Allāh Almighty be pleased with him? [67]

[67] *Khulāṣah al-Fatāwā, Kitāb al-Shahādāt, al-Faṣl al-'Awwal*

Affirmation Precedes Negation

If both methods of establishment are considered insufficient, then one will become deprived of all of the *'awliyā'* of Allāh in all chains, Allāh forbid. Is anyone capable of proving the receipt of *khilāfah* and authorization *('ijāzah)* for every servant of Allāh from their *shaykh*, from the beginning of the chain to the end, by any refined means but himself (the disciple's own claim)? Certainly not! Never! Thus, to negate it necessitates the negation of all chains, Allāh forbid, as you can see.

Moreover, when the chain of successorship and *khilāfah* is proven for Maḥmūd by *shar'ī* (legal) evidence, Ḥāmid bears no right to prevent him from the ceremony of *khirqah-poshī* in the blessed *khānqāh*. Neither the negation of Ḥāmid, nor the negation of anyone, is suitable to be accepted.

It is the consensual principle of the rational and recorded sciences that affirmation takes precedence over negation. If two credible individuals testify that Zayd and Hindah got married, and there are a thousand witnesses for it not occurring, the testification of those thousand negators will surely not be accepted as the essence of it (the negation) is only the negation of one's own knowledge [of an occurrence]. In other words, "It did not take place in our presence," and this does not result in a negation of the occurrence. From the accepted principles is:

المثبت مقدم على النافي لأن من يعلم حجة على من لا يعلم

Affirmation takes precedence over negation as the one who knows is [a source of] evidence above he who does not know.

It is in *al-'Ashbāh*:

بينة النفي غير مقبولة إلا في عشر إلى قوله وفي أيمان
الهداية لا فرق بين أن يحيط علم الشاهد أو لا

The evidence of negation is not accepted except in ten...it is in [the chapter of] Oaths of al-Hidāyah that there is no difference whether the witness knows thoroughly or not.[68]

Why go so far? Just examine the chains of *ṭarīqah* (spirituality). In every chain, by means of 'Imām Ḥasan Baṣarī, there is a link to the Honorable 'Amīr al-Mu'minīn Mawlā 'Alī, may Allāh Almighty ennoble his countenance, although the majority of the *'imāms* of the experts in *Ḥadīth,* who are relied upon in the subject of *Rijāl*[69] and are used as a reference, certainly do not accept him directly hearing from the Honorable Mawlā 'Alī, may Allāh Almighty ennoble his countenance. However, this very principle of rational and recorded sciences:

المثبت مقدم على النافي لأن من حفظ حجة على من لم يحفظ

Affirmation takes precedence over negation because he who remembers is evidence above he who does not remember.

did not allow any disturbance whatsoever in the continuity of the chains. When the negation of such seniors was not accepted in the presence of affirmation, then what impact can the negation of someone of this day and age have?

As for this ceremony not being held for one hundred years due to the stated reason, how can it be admissible as evidence after the successorship being ascertained? The *khirqah-poshī* not taking place for four hundred years on the day of the *'urs* in Ḥāmid's household did not cause it to be impermissible even though this affair did not [previously] exist in his household. Thus, how shall it being practiced continuously in Maḥmūd's household, then it being discontinued for one hundred years due to an excuse, be preventative [of it]?

---

68 *al-'Ashbāh wa al-Naẓā'ir, Kitāb al-Qaḍā' wa al-Shahādāt*

69 *'Ilm al-Rijāl: The study of the states of those found in the chains of transmission of 'aḥādīth (translator)*

An accepted principle of the *sharī'ah* is that:

البقاء أسهل من الابتداء

Continuation is easier than origination.

The 'Amāliqah snatched away the Ark of the Covenant *(Tābūt al-Sakīnah)* from the Banū 'Isrā'īl and it returned after much time. Thus, was their right to seek blessings *(tabarruk)* from it taken away?

Allāh Almighty says:

وَقَالَ لَهُمْ نَبِيُّهُمْ إِنَّ آيَةَ مُلْكِهِ أَنْ يَأْتِيَكُمُ التَّابُوتُ فِيهِ سَكِينَةٌ مِنْ رَبِّكُمْ

And their Prophet said to them, "Indeed, a sign of his kingship is that the Ark shall come to you wherein there is tranquility from your Lord." [70]

Or when the forsaken Qarmatians snatched away the *Ḥajar 'Aswad* from the revered *Ka'bah* and took it to Hajar, and was retrieved by the Muslims, by the grace of Allāh Almighty, twenty-two years later – does the right of the people of *'Islām* or the people of the Sacred House to seek blessings and perform *'istilām* cease to exist therein?

These are clear matters, utterly manifest and evident.

Justice is the best of qualities. ***Allāh Almighty knows best.***

---

[70] *Sūrah al-Baqarah: 248*

The Sixth Question

THE SIXTH QUESTION

Conditions of a Shaykh

QUERY EIGHTY-FOUR

What do the scholars of the religion say concerning upon whose hands is it permissible to pledge allegiance and upon whose hands is it impermissible? Moreover, who possesses the merit to be a *shaykh* [of *ṭarīqah*]?

Apart from this, if the individual who does not possess the merit to take allegiance takes the allegiance of someone, what is the ruling in his favor?

THE ANSWER

Four conditions are necessary to take allegiance and to ascend the throne of guidance:

I. The first being that he be a *sunnī* of sound creed *(ṣaḥīḥ al-'aqīdah)* because the misguided are the hounds of the hellfire and the most inferior creation as it has appeared in the *ḥadīth.*

II. The second being that he be learned of the obligatory knowledge as the unlearned cannot recognize Allāh.

III. The third being that he abstains from major sins as to scorn the sinner *(fāsiq)* is *wājib* (necessary) and it is necessary to revere the *shaykh.* How can the two (scorning and revering) come together?

IV. The fourth being that he possesses authentic and continuous authorization *('ijāzah ṣaḥīḥah muttaṣilah)* as the people of spirituality have consensually agreed upon.

If an individual lacks any one of these conditions, he shall not be taken as a *shaykh.*

Allāh Almighty knows best.

The Seventh Question

THE SEVENTH QUESTION

Singularity of a Shaykh

QUERY EIGHTY-FIVE *Rabī al-Ākhir Sharīf 8, 1315 H.*

What do the scholars of the religion say in the following matter:

'Aḥmad is the disciple and servant of a *walī* of Allāh, an *'imām* of the era. He also possesses authorization *('ijāzah)* from and is licensed *(ma'dhūn)* by the aforementioned *'imām*. After the blessed passing of his *shaykh*, may Allāh be pleased with him, 'Aḥmad thought to renew his allegiance due to excessively sinning. 'Aḥmad had seen in some of the writings of his noble *mashā'ikh*, may Allāh be pleased with them, that if he is unable to access the *shaykh* due to his passing away or due to distance, and he desires the renewal of allegiance *(tajdīd* of *bay'ah)*, he shall renew it on the clothing of the *shaykh*. With this in mind, 'Aḥmad requested the garment of the *shaykh*, may Allāh be pleased with him, from Mawlānā Ḥusayn bin Ḥasan, the *khalīfah* and successor of the noble *shaykh*. Mawlānā [Ḥusayn] responded, "When the successor of the *shaykh* is present, what is the need for the garment?"

It also came to 'Aḥmad's mind that in fact, the representation of the successor should be more complete and superior in perfection than that of the garment. With this intention, he pledged allegiance on Mawlānā's hands, but not for a moment did he ever consider anyone except the honorable *walī* of Allāh and the aforementioned *'imām* to be his *shaykh,* and neither did he include the name of any other in the recitation of the pure chain *(shajarah ṭayyibah),* nor did he pen the name of anyone after that of the honorable shaykh in the *shajarahs* (a booklet containing the names of every *shaykh* in the spiritual chain) he gave to those who pledged allegiance to him.

Now, the aforementioned successor is of the idea that due to the previously mentioned renewal, "'Aḥmad is my disciple," whereas in his own opinion, 'Aḥmad remains on his first allegiance.

What is the truth in this case?

'Aḥmad wishes that, if the error in his thinking is proven, he repents and starts afresh by pledging independent allegiance on the hands of Mawlānā. Moreover, if his opinion is correct, what is the evidence from the pure *sharī'ah* that despite 'Aḥmad having pledged allegiance again on the hands of Mawlānā, he is not to be considered a disciple of Mawlānā?

Explain and be rewarded!

THE ANSWER

In the scenario regarding which the question was asked, 'Aḥmad's opinion is correct; he is upon his first allegiance. He will not be regarded a disciple of the aforementioned successor due to the renewal.

فإنما الأعمال بالنيات وإنما لكل امرئ ما نوى

Verily, actions are [judged] according to the intentions, and for everyone is what he intends.[71]

An evident proof for this from the pure *sharī'ah* is the practice of the Honorable Sayyidunā Ṭalḥah, may Allāh be pleased with him, and the statement of the Honorable 'Amīr al-Mu'minīn, 'Imām of the Gnostics, Master of the Muslims, 'Alī al-Murtaḍā, may Allāh Almighty ennoble his noble countenance.

وناهيك بهما قدوة في الدين

Both of them shall suffice you as a guide in the religion.

When the Honorable Ṭalḥah, may Allāh be pleased with him, retracted his *khaṭa' 'ijtihādī*[72] and intended a renewal of allegiance on the Truth[73]-worshipping hands of the Honorable 'Amīr al-Mu'minīn 'Alī, may Allāh Almighty ennoble his countenance, he had been wounded by the hands of an oppressor. He did not bear the strength to reach 'Amīr al-Mu'minīn 'Alī and a soldier from the army of 'Amīr al-Mu'minīn 'Alī, may Allāh ennoble his countenance, passed by. He called unto him, the Honorable

---

[71] *Ṣaḥīḥ al-Bukhārī: 1*

[72] *Khaṭa' 'Ijtihādī: An inaccurate position assumed by a mujtahid by means of independent judgment ('ijtihād) for which he receives one reward instead of the two he would have received for assuming the accurate position (translator)*

[73] *Truth: al-Ḥaqq, a name of Allāh Almighty (translator)*

Ṭalḥah, may Allāh be pleased with him, renewed the allegiance on his hands, and the sacred soul reached the sacred proximity of Allāh's mercy. Upon hearing this state, 'Amīr al-Mu'minīn 'Alī, may Allāh ennoble his countenance, said:

أبى الله أن يدخل طلحة الجنة إلا وبيعتي في عنقه

Allāh refused to admit Ṭalḥah into Paradise
except while my allegiance is on his neck.[74]

Look! 'Amīr al-Mu'minīn regarded this allegiance as his own allegiance and not that of the soldier, and the Honorable Ṭalḥah had only considered 'Amīr al-Mu'minīn to be the commander of the faithful and worthy of allegiance and not, Allāh forbid, the soldier.

ذلك برهانان من ربك وقد عرضته على محقق الشريعة والطريقة مولانا محب الرسول
عبد القادر القادري البدايوني حفظه الله تعالى عن شر كل مجوني وفتوني فأقره وصوبه
واستحسنه وأعجبه والله سبحانه وتعالى أعلم وعلمه جل مجده أتم وأحكم

Those are two proofs from your Lord. I have presented it to the researcher of the *sharī'ah* and the *ṭarīqah*, Mawlānā Muḥibb al-Rasūl 'Abd al-Qādir al-Qādirī al-Badāyūnī, may Allāh Almighty safeguard him from the evil of all the shameless and those who bring tribulation. He enforced it, deemed it accurate, complimented it, and found it to be astonishing.

Allāh – glory be to Him Almighty – is more knowing, and His knowledge – glorious is its honor – is more perfect and wise.

---

[74] *al-Mustadrak li al-Ḥākim: 5601*

The Eighth Question

THE EIGHTH QUESTION

A Female Cannot be a Shaykh

QUERY EIGHTY-SIX *Shawwāl 20, 1314 H.*

Sent by: Muḥammad 'Aḥmad Khān Ṣāḥib

If a woman, who is pious, acts upon the *sharī'ah*, and is familiar with the *ṭarīqah*, begins taking the allegiance of women and men on her hands, then, from the aspect of *ṭarīqah* and *sharī'ah*, is this allegiance valid or not? Please write the reference of a book alongside the text.

From Jalandhar, Muḥallah Rāstah

THE ANSWER

It is the consensus of the noble *'awliyā'* that the one inviting to Allāh must be a male. Thus, from the pious predecessors to now, no woman has become a *shaykh* and nor has she taken allegiance.

His Luminous Eminence, the Master of the Universe, may Allāh send blessings and salutations upon him, states:

لن يفلح قوم ولوا أمرهم امرأة

A nation who has appointed a woman as their leader shall never succeed.[75]

The *'imāms* 'Aḥmad, Bukhārī, Tirmidhī, and Nasā'ī narrated it from 'Abū Bakrah, may Allāh be pleased with him.

The Gnostic of Allāh, 'Imām Sayyidī 'Abd al-Wahhāb Sha'rānī, may his secret be sanctified, says in *Mīzān al-Sharī'ah, Kitāb al-'Aqḍīyah:*

قد أجمع أهل الكشف على اشتراط الذكورة في كل داع إلى الله تعالى ولم يبلغنا أن أحدا من نساء السلف الصالح تصدرت لتربية المريدين أبدا لنقص النساء في الدرجة وإن ورد الكمال في بعضهن كمريم بنت عمران وآسية امرأة فرعون فذلك كمال بالنسبة للتقوى والدين لا بالنسبة للحكم بين الناس وتسليكهم في مقامات الولاية وغاية أمر المرأة تكون عابدة وزاهدة كرابعة العدوية

The people of divine inspiration agree upon the necessity of being a male in every caller to Allāh. It has not reached us that anyone of the women of the pious predecessors ever took on the [task of] training of the disciples due to the imperfection of women in rank although perfection has manifested in some of them, such as Maryam bint 'Imrān and 'Āsiyah, the wife of

[75] *Ṣaḥīḥ al-Bukhārī: 7099, Jāmi' al-Tirmidhī: 2262, Sunan al-Nasā'ī: 5388, Musnad 'Aḥmad bin Ḥanbal: 20402*

Fir'awn. That was perfection in relation to rulership amongst the people or to guidance in the stations of wilāyah. The extent of a woman's affair is her being a [devout] worshipper and an ascetic like Rābi'ah al-'Adawīyah [al-Baṣarīyah].[76]

والله سبحانه وتعالى أعلم وعلمه جل مجده أتم وأحكم. فقط.

Allāh – glory be to Him Almighty – is more knowing, and His knowledge – glorious is its honor – is more perfect and wise. **End.**

[76] *al-Mizān al-Kubrā, Kitāb al-'Aqḍīyah, Ḥukm Tawlīyah al-Mar'ah al-Qaḍā'*

TheSunniWay

www.ingramcontent.com/pod-product-compliance
Lightning Source LLC
Chambersburg PA
CBHW051323120626
46547CB00015B/2368
* 9 7 8 1 9 5 7 7 7 3 1 9 3 *